Techniques of
Job
Search

CANFIELD PUBLICATIONS IN

BUSINESS COMMUNICATION

Lucian Spataro, Editor

Ohio University

Techniques of
Job
Search

Ross Figgins

California State Polytechnic University, Pomona

Canfield Press
San Francisco
A Department of Harper & Row, Publishers, Inc.
New York   Hagerstown   London

Library of Congress Cataloging in Publication Data

Figgins, Ross.
    Techniques of job search.

    (Canfield publications in business communication)
    Bibliography: p.
    Includes index.
    1. Applications for positions. I. Title.
HF5383.F5   650'.14   76-20555
ISBN 0-06-453708-0

    77 78 79   10 9 8 7 6 5 4 3 2

Contents

Preface

Official government figures indicate that a significant percentage of the eligible workforce is seeking employment, and there is no sign that this number will drop appreciably in the next few years. Most college students are unprepared for this situation. Unless they take a course in business communication, they do not have an opportunity to study the process of finding a job. It seems incongruous that one may spend years preparing for a position but virtually no time studying the basic methods of obtaining it. In recent years, many far-sighted colleges and universities, spurred no doubt by placement statistics, have begun teaching special one- or two-unit classes—open to all majors regardless of academic background—in this critical process.

Techniques of Job Search is designed as a practical reference handbook and textbook. It addresses itself to specific questions and offers practical solutions within the structural context of a complete employment program. Without being prescriptive, it attempts to combine current communication theory, management principles, and, from psychology, field theory, in a useful framework of solutions to common problems faced by applicants.

USES FOR THE BOOK

This book has been prepared for a maximum applicability to various learning situations. It may be used as a supplementary text, as the central resource in a special course in employment, or as a practical reference for any student wanting information and advice about finding a job:

1. As a *supplementary text* for that unit in a business communication course dealing with the problem of securing a job. This use is especially appropriate since most standard texts in the field devote only a small portion to this subject. The text has been designed so that all or only part of the material may be used without a loss in continuity.

2. As the *central text* for a short course, seminar, or workshop focusing on the topic of placement.

3. As a *reference handbook* in a self-instructional program, providing the individual with an orderly and productive plan of operation. This application is especially valuable to anyone who has had little previous experience in the field of business communication or in the employment process and to anyone who wants to improve his or her communication skills in this area.

SPECIAL FEATURES

Some of the special features of this work are:

1. A chronological structure based on an analysis of job placement as a process of communication.

2. A step-by-step discussion of each response required of the applicant, both written and oral.

3. Actual models of written messages that the reader may adapt and use.

4. Examples of poor letters and resumes for comparison, with explanations of how they could be improved.

5. A detailed analysis of each communiqué an applicant may need in terms of content, structure, and purpose.

6. Communication strategies to acquaint the applicant with the employer's perspective, desires, and motivations.

7. A straightforward discussion of common pitfalls and problems, with suggested solutions for overcoming them.

8. A series of specific checklists summarizing various stages of the process.

9. Special discussions on decision-making situations, such as qualifying job leads, negotiating for salary, and deciding whether or not to accept an offer.

10. Progessive exercises, which allow those who elect to use them to work with the concepts described in each chapter while preparing personalized resumes and letters of application.

11. An extensive bibliography of standard references to aid the reader in discovering additional information about employment procedures, the job market, and prospective employers.

12. A writing style and level of language appropriate to any adult audience. No prerequisite courses are necessary to benefit from this book.

ORGANIZATION OF THE BOOK

The text follows the steps of a normal job search, from first contact to last, and analyzes each in terms of its communication opportunities. The Introduction presents an overview of the process and explains the advantages of an organized approach to the task. Succeeding chapters are arranged chronologically and may be handled as independent teaching units. The amount of classroom time required for each will, of course, vary according to the students' needs and the nature of the course in which the book is used. Each chapter is also a relatively discrete discussion of that topic, so that chapters can be reordered or even deleted to meet special instructional needs.

Chapter 1 is about research—where job leads are found and how they are analyzed. The chapter also deals with sources of information about a company or organization, as supplementary information is often required during later stages in the process.

Chapter 2 is a detailed consideration of the resume: its general organization and the selection of information for inclusion. Other related items in this chapter include visual aspects of the resume, model layouts, references, and expanded prose formats.

Chapter 3 completes the first stage of the placement process: finding a potential employer and preparing an application package. This chapter analyzes letters of application: their form, content, and relationship to both the resume and the job description. The chapter is designed to aid the reader in developing professional letter-writing skills. It explores the fundamentals of purpose, structure, physical layout, and mechanics, as well as strategies of negotiation.

Chapter 4 moves to the second stage of job search, the personal interview, and shifts the communication emphasis from written to oral messages. It explains the basic techniques and concerns of an interviewer or company representative: favorable personal qualities, education, background, and experience-related questions, and the use of structure or stress during the meeting. Interspersed with this analysis are suggestions to the applicant on how to respond effectively to various situations.

Chapter 5 concludes the job-search process with an explanation of the need and uses of various second-order written communiqués. The chapter deals with various forms of follow-up letters, inquiries, negotiations, and other supplementary messages. It also contains suggested aids, such as a mailing log and a decision-analysis chart, to help the applicant in handling such important factors as timing and focus.

The text concludes with an extensive bibliography of further resources to assist in the satisfactory culmination of the employment process.

In summary, *Techniques of Job Search* analyzes each stage of applying for a job in terms of its communication requirements and presents sample responses. The fundamental principle that governs the book's practical use is flexibility in meeting an individual's specific needs by studying the situation and applying the suggestions presented.

ACKNOWLEDGMENTS

This book was written with the advice and assistance of many people. I am unable to list all of them here, but wish to thank those who have been particularly helpful during the preparation of the manuscript. Therefore, at the risk of leaving someone out, I thank the American Business Communication Association, *ABCA Bulletin* editor George H. Douglas and members of his staff, Alfred Sheldon, Leonard Franco, Carole Myrick, Louise Strona, and James V. Shepard. I also wish to thank Professors F. D. Nott, of the University of Arizona, and Lucian Spataro, of Ohio University, for their helpful reviews of the manuscript Many of their suggestions have been incorporated in the text. Special thanks go to my wife, Jacque Weiss, for her support and encouragement. I am also grateful to the faculty of the Communication Arts Department and California State Polytechnic University, Pomona, for endorsing the sabbatical leave during which I prepared this book.

Introduction

A Program for Employment

How should I look for a new job?
What are the steps involved?
Where should I begin?

The time and effort you spend in looking for a good job represent a considerable investment in your future. But the process can be very trying emotionally if you go through it without help. This book is a step-by-step guide to the job-search process. It is intended to help you look for a job intelligently and obtain a position that matches your skills and background. The book encourages you to adapt your efforts to the realities of the job market and present a responsible image to a potential employer. Above all, it instructs you in constructing the best possible employment-application package.

Finding the right job takes time and requires a personal commitment. The process is composed of a number of specific steps:

1. Research of the job market
2. Preparation of the application package
   a. Resumes
   b. Application letters
   c. Follow-up letters
3. Interview with employer
4. Response to hiring offer

In a competitive employment situation, convincing a potential employer of your value depends on your ability to communicate your qualifications articulately and self-confidently. This book is designed to help you plan your communication effectively at each stage of the job-search process. Each chapter discusses requirements and techniques relevant to a specific stage and provides model letters and resumes based on different hypothetical situations. You are encouraged to return to these models when preparing your application package and to use the text and accompanying checklists in modifying the models to suit your needs. The result will be an individualized and effective package reflecting your own situation.

1

Each chapter begins with a list of the questions most frequently asked by job seekers. The answers to these questions form the bulk of the text. At the end of each chapter is a series of exercises designed to reinforce your understanding of the principles discussed. These exercises take two forms: discussion topics relating to the questions at the beginning of the chapter, and project topics drawn from actual situations. Some of the projects require role-playing activities. You are urged to involve your imagination as freely as possible in these activities, since learning to play a role well can increase your ability to handle similar situations as well as your confidence. The overall goal of the exercises is to improve your communication skills so you can open lines of communication between yourself and potential employers.

Chapter 1, on research, covers techniques of finding and evaluating job leads. The reader is instructed in how to collect information for use in judging leads and selecting appropriate firms.

Chapter 2 deals with the most fundamental written item in the job-search process--the personal resume. The reader will learn how to write a personal resume and how to use it in relation to specific jobs. Letters of recommendation are also covered in this chapter.

Chapter 3 is based on the premise that an application is strengthened when a letter accompanies the resume to form a complete package. The application letter is analyzed here and, as with the resume, the reader is instructed in developing an application suitable to his or her own situation. Specific writing problems that might arise in such letters are also considered in Chapter 3.

Chapter 4 considers the personal interview, the crucial face-to-face meeting between an applicant and a potential employer. This chapter analyzes the interview from both the perspective of the interviewer and that of the applicant. Applicants are encouraged to remember that the nature and purpose of the interview from the interviewer's perspective is to search out the best-qualified people for the organization. Interviewees can thus prepare themselves accordingly and reduce the anxiety of facing an unknown series of questions. The simulation exercises at the end of this unit are particularly important. They are designed to demonstrate various interviewing techniques and warn against common pitfalls.

Chapter 5 covers the final stage of the job-search process, concentrating particularly on the crucial, and frequently overlooked, follow-up phase. In a recent survey, personnel directors and recruiters were asked to rate the effectiveness of the follow-up letter; their responses ranged from neutral to strongly positive. Not one of these professionals felt that a letter received after the interview would disqualify an applicant. A well-prepared series of auxiliary messages may not only help the applicant to secure employment, but also may supplement negotiations for increased benefits. This chapter covers the range of situations in which additional letters might prove useful. Also discussed is a method of decision making based on a simplified form of systems analysis, designed to help an applicant recognize and weigh the importance of a number of dissimilar items simultaneously.

The appendices contain material selected to supplement the student's understanding of the employment process, sample application forms, and a list of two-letter abbreviations for the fifty states. The bibliography, the final element in the book, lists recent sources of specialized information on the job-search process.

Research 1

Not Just Any Job Will Do

What kind of job am I looking for?
Where will I find good leads?
Who can I ask for help?
How can I find out which companies are hiring?
What are employment agencies? Should I hire one?
How should I arrange the information I collect?

Some people are fortunate: They can open a newspaper one morning and, after a few telephone calls, find just the job they wanted. But job seekers and job descriptions rarely match up this quickly. A glance through any newspaper's classified section reveals a bewildering number of job notices (see Figure 1.1). Even deciding which employers to contact requires study and evaluation. A job seeker must gather information for use at every step of the game: judging job leads, evaluating prospective employers, and actually applying for a desired position.

A PERSONAL JOB DESCRIPTION

A successful job application is one which matches a qualified individual with a specific position. At the very start of the job-search process the job seeker should have a solid idea of the kind of position he or she is looking for. This aspect of seeking employment is the most personal, since it requires self-knowledge and a sense of individual priorities. After all, careers are not built on paychecks. What are your values and personal characteristics? How do they influence your idea of a satisfying job? You can begin to answer these general questions—which will continue to be relevant as long as you are employed—by carefully weighing your answers to some more specific ones:

1. How important is salary?
2. What am I qualified to do?
3. What job conditions suit me best?
4. What are my personal strengths? weaknesses?
5. Do I have any special skills?
6. Do I like to work with other people?

FIGURE 1.1. Classified ads from newspapers.

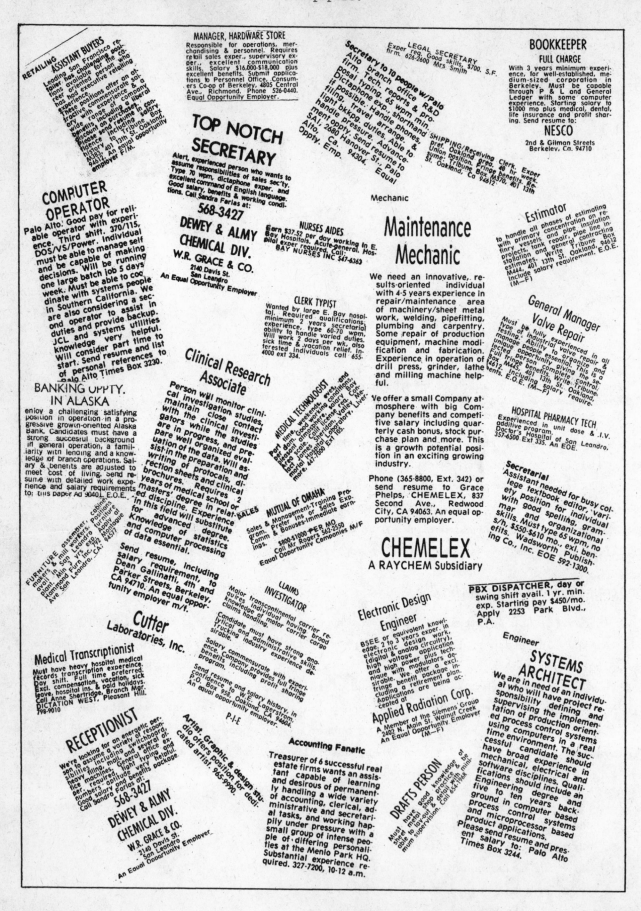

4

7. How do I see my professional future?

8. Why should someone hire me?

9. How much am I worth to an employer?

10. Is this job really for me?

Those questions are not easy to answer. But in thinking about them honestly you will learn to approach prospective jobs with sincerity, eventually developing a yardstick by which to measure your interest in a job. Also a firm understanding of your personal job requirements will help you to negotiate a final agreement once an offer is made.

USING THE EMPLOYER'S DESCRIPTION

In your search for leads, try to obtain the most detailed job descriptions possible. The samples in Figures 1.2 through 1.4, demonstrate that an increasing amount of information is presented as you progress from classified advertisements through job summaries or briefs, and finally to formal job descriptions. Ads are only abbreviations; they are designed to put you in contact with a company for further information. If you are not able to obtain a more detailed description of an advertised position by phoning or writing the advertiser, you may have to find an ad—from another source which uses the same job title. You can then deduce the nature of the former from what you learn about the latter.

An employer's notice of an opening, no matter how detailed, usually provides only the most basic information—job title, salary, education, and experience requirements, and the address of the organization advertising. But an applicant should learn to read a job description for other important clues in how to apply.

A full job description is above all a checklist for the applicant. Information you uncover at this stage can be applied throughout the process: in preparing the resume and letter of application, during the interview, and eventually in evaluating an offer. Study the description carefully and underline the major qualifications; then make sure you discuss these points in your application. Also, use the advertiser's terminology when describing your own qualifications. Finally, read the description carefully and see if you can picture the ideal applicant. Compare this image with your personal job description. How closely do they match? The closer the fit, the better the job lead is for you.

But do not become discouraged and discard a lead automatically if the "fit" is not exact. The employment description is primarily a guide, prepared by an organization to aid itself in selecting the best person for a certain task. It is not an absolute measure of any particular individual, but an explanation of the job to be done in terms of the skills required to do it. It is also the first step in a sophisticated process of information exchange: Potential employers use advertisements, job descriptions and sometimes even telephone messages to tell you, the potential applicant, what they are seeking. You in turn explain to them, through resumes, letters of application, and your responses in interviews, how closely you can meet those needs. Adjustments of expectations can be, and often are, made during the process on both sides.

FIGURE 1.2. A job summary from a
professional journal.

DIRECTOR OF FOUNDATION SERVICES

Medium-sized university needs a qualified
person with overall administrative experience to supervise its related services
functions. Degree and experience
required. Send resume and salary requirements to Hazel Lopez, Personnel Officer,
Unit Foundation, 1212 University Center,
Harrisburg, PA 17105.

FIGURE 1.3. A job brief from an employment bulletin.

CURRENT JOB OPENING

DIRECTOR OF FOUNDATION SERVICES

Salary: $1854 to 2253/month

Bachelor's degree in Business Administration. Five years experience in
administrative positions. Knowledge of various management techniques.
Ability to supervise others, make decisions, write well, and establish cooperative working relations with diverse groups. Accounting background also
desirable. Duties include multiple role of administrator, analyst and
advisor to the Board of Directors. Anticipated date for position to commence:
February 1. Salary will be commensurate with experience and level of expertise. Send resume and salary requirements to Hazel Lopez, Personnel Officer,
Unit Foundation, 1212 University Center, Harrisburg, PA 17105.

FIGURE 1.4. Job description.

CURRENT JOB OPENING

UNIT FOUNDATION, INC.
City University
Harrisburg, PA 17105

SEND RESUME TO:
Hazel Lopez, Personnel Officer
Unit Foundation, Inc.
1212 University Center
Harrisburg, PA 17105

DIRECTOR OF FOUNDATION SERVICES--------------------------$1854 - 2253/month

INTRODUCTION

The Unit Foundation, Inc. is a self-supporting auxiliary organization charged with the responsibility of providing auxiliary services on a university campus of 10,000 students. The Foundation has approximately 110 staff employees and approximately 250 student employees during the academic year.

TYPICAL TASKS

Responsible to the Board of Directors of the Unit Foundation, Inc. for the overall administration of the Foundation which includes the campus bookstore, all university food service operations, Foundation accounting services and the personnel program of the Foundation.

MINIMUM QUALIFICATIONS

Education: Bachelor's degree in Business Administration or equivalent.

Experience: Five years experience in progressively responsible administrative positions. Must have significant supervisory experience.

Knowledge: Thorough knowledge of current management techniques; ability to plan, organize and direct the work of others; ability to analyze data and draw sound conclusions; ability to prepare clear and concise reports; ability to establish and maintain cooperative work relationships with campus administrators, faculty, staff and students. Knowledge of accounting principles highly desirable.

Personal: Highly motivated individual with strengths in interpersonal relations and ability to deal tactfully in sensitive situations essential to the service orientation of the Foundation.

Anticipated date for position to commence: February 1, 1976.

ALL QUALIFIED APPLICANTS WILL RECEIVE CONSIDERATION
FOR EMPLOYMENT WITHOUT REGARD TO RACE, CREED, NATIONAL ORIGIN, OR SEX.

INITIAL RESEARCH: FINDING JOB LEADS

Every job is related to the climate of the employment market in the particular field and at a particular time. Some job categories shift more drastically over time than others, so it is advisable that you get a feel for the employment trend in your particular field now. Is there mobility—that is, does the field offer opportunities for employees to advance? Are leads going to be easy or hard to find? Sometimes a survey of the number of jobs offered in the Sunday classifieds will suffice. Simply determine whether the section has grown or shrunk over a several-month period. For a more definitive indication, check a current employment-statistic reference in your library; see, for example, *Employment and Wages in the United States*, or published reports of the Bureau of Labor Statistics. You should also consult colleagues, personnel directors, government agencies, counselors, or anyone else who might be sensitive to trends in your field. Don't hesitate to ask questions. Job markets can be very difficult to analyze, and questions often lead you to sound information; they could even lead to a job.

Many different sources of employment leads exist. The following is an overview of the major sources:

1. Periodicals
   a. Newspapers and magazines
   b. Professional journals
   c. Trade journals and yearbooks

2. Agencies and Services
   a. Government agencies: federal, state, and local
   b. Employment agencies
   c. College placement services
   d. Professional organizations

3. Letters of Inquiry

4. Advertising oneself (Situations Wanted)

As you explore these sources for job information, keep in mind that the source of a job lead is related to the location of the job. Therefore, a publication originating in New York will probably tell you more about opportunities in that city than anywhere else. The further away from home you go to find a position, the greater the chance that you will have to consider moving to a new locale.

PERIODICALS

Newspapers and Magazines

The newspaper—local, metropolitan, or national—is the medium most widely used for advertising employment situations. Newspapers are therefore a good starting point in any placement program. Begin by reading the section that applies to your field of interest for an impression of the job market. Take note of the size of the ads, salary ranges, and the number and location of situations offered. From these indicators you can gain a sense of the current need for your skills. Keep a list of the positions that look promising, and save the advertisement for reference.

Don't limit yourself to the classified section, however. Read any articles throughout the paper about companies that may hire in your field. After all, the name of a company is all you have to know to make an inquiry. If you read an announcement of a new contract, you might be able to write for employment information before the company even advertises for additional employees.

Many newspapers, among them the *New York Times* and the *Los Angeles Times*, periodically print a placement supplement or an employment insert. These special sections are usually crammed with useful information, advertisements, articles, services, book reviews, and advice—all intended to aid the job seeker and attract inquiries.

Most magazines are meant to appeal to specific audiences, so their classified sections do not reflect the total employment picture in their places of origin. Also, their classified ad sections are more selective and usually more expensive than those of newspapers. But advertisements in magazines can be of great value to job-seekers looking for specific types of jobs related to an individual magazine's point of view or field of interest. Also valuable are the employment guides often advertised in the classified sections of national magazines. They catalogue such information as employment opportunities overseas or employment opportunities in specific fields. Such publications do not necessarily list job openings, but they do provide a source of names and addresses for writing inquiries.

If you are interested in writing to newspapers or magazines in other areas for copies, look up their addresses in *Ayer's Directory of Newspapers and Periodicals*

Professional Journals

In virtually every professional field at least one association exists which issues a journal of interest to its members. These periodicals primarily publish articles updating relevant information, but some do contain classified sections advertising employment opportunities. Journals are also useful for their announcements of professional meetings, conventions, seminars, and conferences where job seekers can make contact with potential employers in person. To find the address of an association in your field, check the *Encyclopedia of Associations* (which lists 1,400 groups) or *Scientific and Technical Societies and Institutions of the United States and Canada*. Most libraries carry these reference works.

Another means of tracking down professional journals are publication indices, specialized reference works which list the titles of articles and publications in specific professional fields. You will find the names of many periodicals in these indices; jot them down and look up their addresses in *Ayer's Directory*. Some examples of widely circulated indices are *The Accountant's Index*, *Applied Science and Technology Index*, *The Art Index*, *Biological and Agricultural Index*, *Business Periodicals Index*, *Education Index*, *Engineering Index*, and *Industrial Arts Index*. As you go through these indices for the names of journals, look through the titles of current articles. Quite often special articles or editorials are prepared on the employment situation in a particular profession. An analysis of this kind can be a goldmine of information.

Trade Journals and Yearbooks

Trade journals and yearbooks are usually published by a single company or industrial group; they are specialized sources of information concerning that company or industry. These publications are similar to professional journals in that they do not necessarily advertise for employees, but by skimming through them you can learn which companies are doing what and where to write for further information.

A standard reference source for trade journals, newspapers, and yearbooks is the *Gebbie Press House Magazine Directory*; it lists four thousand business periodicals in the United States. A second resource is the *Writer's Market*. This annual reference guide for writers lists and describes five thousand specialized magazines and journals. You will discover some truly esoteric listings in these two source books—for example, the *Western Livestock Journal, Mobile Home Park Management and Developer Magazine, Optical Journal and Review of Optometry, Drycleaning World,* and *Civil Service Labor Directory*

AGENCIES AND SERVICES

Government—Federal, State, and Local

The United States federal government is the largest employer in the nation, and is a rich source of leads for job seekers in every field. For information concerning job openings contact the Federal Personnel and Management Office or the U.S. Civil Service Commission. Both agencies maintain local branch offices in major cities as well as central offices in Washington, D.C. You may also contact any local office of the federal government. They are listed in the telephone directory under "United States Government."

The Veterans Administration, through its special employment and placement programs, aids military and former military personnel in finding jobs and training. If you are in the military and plan to return to civilian life in the near future, contact your commander's office for information concerning civilian employment training and placement. Former service personnel should call the local Veterans Administration office or see their campus representative.

The federal government also requires each state to maintain a referral office for employment. Originally these offices were simply called unemployment bureaus, but today most states have given them more pleasing titles, such as Employment Development Agency or Department of Human Resources. To find your local agency consult the telephone directory under the name of your state. For example, look under "Rhode Island, State of" or "California, State Offices." These state employment offices are referral services for general employment throughout the community. (Most federal and local government personnel offices are primarily interested in hiring for their own needs.) Besides issuing and regulating unemployment insurance and workers' compensation, state employment agencies offer extensive job listings and employment counseling services.

County and city governments maintain personnel offices for their own hiring requirements. They also keep files of job referrals from other levels of government. Call your local City Hall for further information about employment listings.

Employment Agencies

An employment agency is a commercial organization in business to help people find jobs. (Nonprofit employment agencies do exist, but they are usually associated with institutions, professional organizations, or special civic programs.) Normally these companies provide a job seeker with employment leads, career counseling, and assistance in developing a personal application package. For these services they usually charge the applicant a fixed fee or a percentage of the salary when he or she is placed, although sometimes the employer pays the fee. If you decide to hire an employment agency to help you find a position, be sure to find out first what services they offer and how much they will cost. This advice is especially important if the agency requires you to sign a contract, since the terms of the binding agreement may be unacceptable. For example, the contract may commit you to paying more of your first month's salary than you are able to afford. If you do hire an agency and take a job on their referral, remember to notify them immediately.

College Placement Services

If you are a college graduate, contact your alumni association or write directly to the campus placement office asking whether their services are available to you. Most colleges and universities maintain a placement service that lists current openings on and off campus. Some of these offices also keep reference files for graduates and arrange interviews with industry recruiters. Ask the college placement counselor for a copy of the current *College Placement Annual*, a publication that lists the occupational requirements and addresses of fifteen hundred corporate and government employers.

Professional Organizations

Some professional groups, including trade unions, maintain placement or referral services for their membership. A letter of inquiry to the association most closely allied with your field of interest could bring you some excellent advice and put you in contact with a number of prospective employers. The advantage of these sources is that any listing you receive will have been screened. But keep in mind that these services are usually reserved for active members.

To identify associations related to your field, consult the reference books listed in the sections headed "Professional Journals" and "Trade Journals and Yearbooks" above. For example, if you are interested in college teaching, you would look in the *Education Index* and find *Placement Services for Personnel in Higher Education*. *Placement Services*, which contains information on 112 related organizations, might lead you to the *ASCUS Annual* (published by the Association for School, College and University Staffing) or the *Chronicle of Higher Education*. Both publications list placement bureaus and advertise current vacancies in the field.

LETTERS OF INQUIRY

Letters of inquiry are general requests for information. They are not accompanied by resumes, but are simply letters asking direct questions: "Does your company need anyone with my skills now? If not, might a need develop in the near future?" The advantage of the inquiry approach is that it enlarges your employment spectrum. You need not limit yourself to advertisers, but can send an inquiry to any company that interests you. If you receive an encouraging reply to an inquiry, you can send an application immediately. As a matter of fact, an inquiry letter often evokes more feedback than an application; you may request an immediate response in the former, while the latter might be filed away for future reference and elicit no response at all.

An inquiry is similar to an application (see Chapter 3), but is usually more general. It tends to outline the writer's field of experience without citing dates and without referring to a specific job. Notice in Figure 1.5 that the applicant is not a specialist; her general and diverse background could be successfully utilized in numerous positions within a company. The inquiry method is particularly well-suited to job seekers with such backgrounds, since they are able to adapt to different jobs that might exist.

The woman in the example is using the inquiry letter to discover whether her experience might be useful to the company. The most encouraging response she could hope for would be a list of specific job titles for which she could apply. The inquiry technique is quite useful if one is seeking employment with a certain kind of company in a specific area. One need only open the phone book or other directory and begin to send out inquiries. The disadvantage of this approach is that it takes time and delays the application by one step.

ADVERTISING FOR "SITUATIONS WANTED"

Some job hunters take the initiative beyond letters of inquiry and actually advertise for themselves (see Figure 1.6). Self-advertising is not commonly used by college graduates looking for their first position. This technique has its best return among more experienced professionals.

The potential benefits of self-advertising must be balanced against the cost of running the ad. Taking out ads, even small ones, can be expensive, particularly if the ads run for some time. Therefore, even though the costs may be deductible from your taxes later, you may not wish to gamble against the chance that the ad will not pay off with some solid leads.

If you do decide to advertise, take account of the following factors to maximize your ad's potential: the amount of money you can afford to spend; the size and character of the publication's intended audience; and the size, style, and layout—that is, the graphic impact—of the ad itself.

Read the "Situations Wanted" columns in a few large newspapers before writing the final copy for your advertisement. Keep the message brief and precise. A condensation of the best points from your letter of application should work very well here. Do not rely heavily on abbreviations; they may save money, but they can be confusing and detract from the ad's purpose.

THE SECOND STEP: INVESTIGATING YOUR LEADS

Preparing a list of employment leads is a two-part task:

1. Find out about job openings currently available—that is, locate the targets.
2. Identify the employers and determine whether the target positions really interest you—in other words, qualify your leads.

The first step in this process is obvious, but the second is often overlooked. Such an oversight could lead you to waste a significant amount of time and energy. For example, you might get all the way to the interview stage before discovering that the position is not what you wanted at all.

The guiding principle in evaluating leads is relatively simple: A good lead is one in which the job offered matches your personal idea of a good job. A poor one would require you to sacrifice too much of what you are looking for without compensating you adequately.

To evaluate the nature of a lead fully, though, you must have some specific information about the company or organization offering the job. A number of sourcebooks on American business and industry are available in the reference section of most libraries. Consult a trade directory to

FIGURE 1.5. A letter of inquiry.

505 West 44th Street
New York, NY 10037

September 8, 1976

Ms. R. L. Thatcher
  Personnel Director
Thomas Sportswear
700 S. Central Mall
Danbury, CT 06810

Dear Ms. Thatcher:

I know the clothing business!

During the past fifteen years, ever since I graduated from high school, I have been working in the clothing industry. I began as a cutter, and learned the trade from the bottom up. Since then I have been a shop supervisor, a materials buyer, design consultant, and production manager.

Now I am interested in finding a position with a small, but successful company, such as Thomas Sportswear, where I can put my experience and ideas to work. I feel qualified to handle any position related to manufacturing, designing, or purchasing.

Do you have an opening for me?

I will be pleased to supply you with my resume or bring it to a personal interview if your response to this letter is encouraging.

I hope to hear from you in the near future.

Truly yours,

B. Audrey Griffith

B. Audrey Griffth

FIGURE 1.6. Ads for "Situations Wanted." Three are forthright and informative; the fourth is incomprehensible due to overuse of abbreviations.

OVERSEAS BASED EXECUTIVE seeks position in San Francisco or abroad. B.S. in Engineering and M.B.A. Over ten years experience as a management consultant and project manager. Contact . . .

ARCHITECT
Innovative problem solver—14 years varied experience housing, commercial and health-related facilities. Call . . . after 5:00.

CONTROLLER, C.P.A.
Direct All Financial Operations: Statements, Reports, Budgets, Heavy Credit/Collections, Bank Relations. Available Now. Z77704 Times

ACCT Contr exp ad o/m BBA+ F/S Consol An EDP/BUDG Sys CF cr/ coll taxes costs. (213) 449-8811

discover what a company produces, what services it offers, what size it is, and so on. Trade directories are listed in the *Guide to American Directories* or *Trade Directories of the World*. These reference books will direct you to directories listing employers in your field. Examples of trade directories are:

Bradford's Directory of Market Research (lists agencies and individuals engaged in marketing and economic research)

Business Periodicals Index (index to periodicals in accounting, advertising, banking and finance, general business, insurance, labor and management, marketing and purchasing, office management, public administration, taxation, specific businesses, industries, and trades)

College Placement Annual (two overviews of various fields)

Funk and Scott's Index of Corporations and Industries (index to periodical articles and other references on industries and individual corporations)

Moody's Manuals (which divide major American Industry into five categories)

The Occupational Index (index of current publications on occupational information)

Statistics Sources (index of current statistical data arranged by subject)

Thomas' Register of American Manufacturers (A-Z list of leading manufacturers, trade names, and organizations; chambers of commerce, boards of trade)

If you have any difficulty finding information about a company, ask a reference librarian for help, or consult one of the books specifically designed as guides in this kind of research:

14

H. Webster Johnson's *How to Use the Business Library*, the *Small Business Bibliography Series* prepared by the Small Business Administration, or "Employment" in *The Standard Periodical Directory*.

You may wish to learn something about the owners, officers, directors, or founders of an organization. Look up biographical information in *Who's Who*, *Poor's Register of Directors and Executives of the United States and Canada*, and the *Dictionary of American Biography*.

Use the publication indices described earlier to find articles written about the company you are researching. The indices will direct you to stories, features, or editorials in the journals or trade papers. Indices are usually paperbound quarterly and hardbound annually. If the index goes back far enough, and if you are willing to expend a considerable amount of energy, you might be able to trace the entire history of a company or organization.

Do not ignore the less formal methods of informing yourself about an organization. Ask questions of people who might deal with the company and contact current employees. You may also write or telephone the local Chamber of Commerce, the Better Business Bureau, the Small Business Administration, or local newspapers and service organizations. Investigate until you are satisfied that you have an *authentic* picture of your prospective employer.

The information you collect in this research will serve you in three ways:

1. It will allow you to evaluate leads.
2. It will help you to prepare and individualize application packages.
3. It will equip you to discuss the company intelligently in a personal interview.

THE FINAL STAGE: ARRANGING YOUR INFORMATION

When you have gathered sufficient information, make a preferential list of the leads that remain interesting to you, beginning with the most attractive. This list should form a column down the left-hand side of a large piece of paper. The order of the entries will determine the order in which the application packages will eventually be mailed.

You will want your applications to cover the specific requirements of each position, so make a checklist of job requirements for each lead. Determine these requirements from the job description and the information you have collected about the organization. What qualities do you think the organization is looking for in a future employee? What qualifications are implied as well as stated? Write down all the points you can identify for each lead next to the appropriate entry. Discussing all of these items in one application may eventually prove to be impractical, but this information will guide you in preparing the resume and cover letter to suit the job. It will also help you to see your background from the potential employer's point of view.

You may be asking yourself if this detailed list is really necessary. The answer is an unqualified yes if you are intending to tailor your applications to the jobs you want. The easy approach, sending out identical form letters to all potential employers, is the most frequently used, and therefore the least distinctive, job-search method. Also, since your research will presumably have turned up significant differences among possible employers, sending out identical packages would simply delay your opportunity to discuss the target job specifically.

Once your research chores are finished, your list will contain a substantial amount of practical information about employment prospects in your field. Save this data, it could be valuable to you for later reference. By this time you should know a great deal about the job market and the specific kind of job you want. You should also have decided on the organizations you want to work for and why.

EXERCISES

1. Discussion topics:

    a. Why is a personal job description valuable?

    b. What can you learn from reading the classified ads in a newspaper?

    c. What constitutes a lead? A "good lead"? A "bad lead"?

    d. What are the advantages of keeping a preferential list of leads?

    e. What services might a college placement office offer? An employment agency?

    f. What should go into a "Situations Wanted" ad?

    g. Why is a detailed job description valuable?

    h. What can you learn from doing job research?

    i. How can you find out about the job market in a particular field?

2. Search through a recent copy of a local newspaper for all possible job leads *not* listed in the employment section of the classifieds. Follow up on two or three of these leads. What further information do you need? Where can you get it?

3. Prepare a letter of inquiry for a full- or part-time job with the leads you found in Exercise 2.

4. Visit the local state employment agency. Write a review of the agency's services and speculate how best to utilize those services in your own job search.

5. Select two companies listed in the *College Placement Annual* and research them thoroughly. Include biographical information on their executive staff. Outline a procedure for securing a job with them based on your research and your own qualifications.

6. Using the *Gebbie Press House Magazine Directory* or the *Writer's Market*, prepare a list of all existing publications related to the type of employment you are seeking. Decide which seems most promising and send for recent copies for yourself.

7. Is there a placement office on your campus? As a special project, ask your instructor to invite one of their counselors to explain its services to your class.

The Resume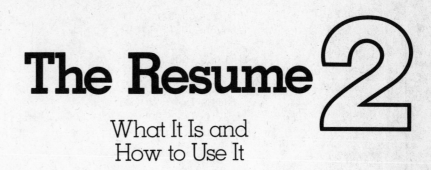
What It Is and
How to Use It

What is a resume?
Do I need one?
What information should my resume contain? Why?
How should the resume be organized?
How should references be handled?
What are the graphic considerations in preparing a resume?

The use of individually prepared resumes—sometimes called personal-data or curriculum sheets, vitae, dossiers, or curriculum vitae—is on a steady increase. At one time only "professionals" sent out personal resumes, but today a wide range of people, from executives to secretaries, are using this tool effectively to help them find employment. (See Figure 2.1.)

A well-constructed resume serves a number of purposes:

1. It organizes information so the reader can grasp it quickly and easily.

2. It is flexible, allowing you to stress your strengths in terms of certain positions.

3. It is a permanent record of your accomplishments.

4. It reduces the possibility of pointless interviews, since it allows an employer to review your qualifications and determine whether or not they match the job requirements.

5. You can cite it in salary negotiations.

6. You can expand your potential job market by mailing it to many possible employers.

7. It is an example of your professional skill and attention to detail.

8. It can accompany your request for a personal interview.

You can expect to present information about yourself at each stage of the job-search process. Naturally, an employer will want to base his or her selection of an employee on the background, experience, and qualifications of the applicants. Many organizations use a standard application form which asks conventional questions about an applicant's history as it may apply to a wide range of positions. (See the sample application forms in Appendix B.) The resume differs from the application form in that it can be developed to address a specific job; the applicant's background may be described in terms of that job alone.

FIGURE 2.1. A sample resume.

Harold E. Kolasinsky

ADDRESS: 5100 Canoga Street
Sheboygan, WI 53081

PHONE: (414) 626-0000

PERSONAL: BIRTH DATE: 2/25/45   MARITAL STATUS: Single
HEIGHT: 6'2"   CITIZENSHIP: USA
WEIGHT: 190   MILITARY STATUS: 1H
HEALTH: Excellent   SOCIAL SECURITY: 505-00-1909

CAREER
OBJECTIVE: I am interested in obtaining a job that will provide general
experience in Civil Engineering.

EDUCATION:

1970-1973 California State Polytechnic University, Pomona

Degree: Bachelor of Science in Civil Engineering
June, 1973

Major: Civil Engineering

1963-1968 Modesto Junior College, Modesto, CA
part-time

Degree: Associate of Arts
June, 1968

Major: Civil Engineering

EXPERIENCE:

1963-1970 U.S. Department of Agriculture—Forest Service
Sonora, CA

Surveying Technician—part-time school year and full-time
summer work as a crew chief on survey party, crew boss
trainee for fire fighting.

HONORS AND
ACTIVITIES: E.I.T.—California 1972
Tau Beta Pi 1973
Varsity Football—M.J.C. 1963

REFERENCES:

John Smith   James Crawford
Assistant Forest Engineer   Associate Professor
Stanislaus National Forest   California State Polytechnic University,
180 East View Way   Pomona
Sonora, CA 95370   3801 West Temple Avenue
Pomona, CA 91768

Portfolio of Civil Engineering designs, prepared at university, is available
for review during interview.

You probably fill many roles in your everyday life; the characteristics and responsibilities for each of these vary widely. Preparing a resume will help you to make an inventory of your diverse experience and abilities and select those features that apply best to a specific job opening. The resume affords you the best opportunity to demonstrate that you fit a position. You are not limited to simply filling in the blanks as on an application form, but can pick and choose the information you wish to provide.

You can benefit from the preparation of a complete resume in a number of other ways as well. First, you will supply yourself with carefully worded summaries of your experience. These summaries will be more complete and reliable than those you might come up with from memory, and they can be used over and over in letters related to hiring, on application forms, and even during interviews. Second, the development of a resume allows you to review your own background objectively in terms of who you are and where you are going. Very often, patterns in a career develop which remain obscure until the job seeker is forced to review his or her experience. Ask yourself what elements your work experience and education have in common. Do these characteristics serve as qualifications for a specific career? Should you be thinking about trying to increase your qualifications? Or perhaps you should change your career goals instead.

The main function of a well-written resume, however, is to present an image of you to a prospective employer—particularly when you are not present to speak on your own behalf. For example, when two or more people with virtually equal qualifications apply for the same position, as happens often, resumes are re-read and the screening process becomes finer. The personnel officer will look again and begin asking tougher questions about each applicant: Do certain details on this person's resume indicate a special ability to accept responsibility? Does she have an inclination toward leadership? Does his background suggest a person who will grow with the organization? In other words, a good resume will identify not only an applicant who has performed well on other jobs, but also one who *will* perform well on a new job. As sincerely as possible, try to determine what your past as outlined in your resume tells someone about your potential. Employers will advance applicants whose resumes and applications most closely match the detailed job description to the personal-interview stage.

Besides a neat appearance, the critical factors in resume writing are selection and emphasis. Good resume writers know they are preparing a flexible summary of their backgrounds. They ask themselves these questions: What should be included? Where should it go? This chapter concentrates on these two considerations. It identifies information appropriate to resumes, and demonstrates successful methods of arranging the material.

THE SELECTION OF INFORMATION

A resume is a summary of your experience, not a full biography. A complete account of your background, even if it could be compiled, would be too cumbersome and cluttered with extraneous information. It would lack the necessary focus, and thus tend to confuse rather than inform the reader. The formula for successful resumes is quite simple: Keep them short and efficient.

Major companies sometimes receive hundreds of applications a day, so your resume will often be competing for attention with a great many others. Therefore, it should sketch your qualifications selectively and clearly in order to convince the reader on the first reading that you deserve careful consideration. Learn to think of your experience from the point of view of the employer. What are his or her needs and interests? How can you construct your resume to relate to those needs and interests? Basically, the material you include should introduce you to the reader from two perspectives: First it should demonstrate that your background suits you for the specific job at hand. Second, it should illustrate other qualities that would benefit the company as a whole.

GENERAL ORGANIZATION

The resume is an *organized* presentation of an applicant's background and experience. For the sake of quick reading and easy understanding, it is normally divided into "blocks" of similar information (see Figure 2.2). No fixed rules exist to say which facts must appear in a resume or how they should be organized, but short blocks of data following brief headings result in an efficient, easy-to-read presentation. The general outline in Figure 2.2 demonstrates that the most frequently presented information breaks down naturally into separate blocks. The outline in the figure is one of several possible formats, but the concept of information blocks is common to them all.

When considering your own background, you will have to decide which facts are most appropriate and informative, and then organize those facts into data blocks. Actually constructing the blocks so that they present the most relevant information efficiently takes some effort. Begin this procedure by studying available job descriptions in your field. Make a brief list of the specific qualifications required for these positions. Notice how quickly this information begins to divide itself into convenient groups, such as experience and education. The writers who prepared the job descriptions were actually writing resumes in miniature. All the resume writer has to do, then, is identify the appropriate categories of information, provide the information that fits these categories, and add supplementary information that will further support the stated requirements.

Ask yourself these key questions:

1. What qualifications are required for this position?
2. What qualifications are mentioned as desirable?
3. What qualifications of mine which are not mentioned specifically would be helpful in this job?

Your answers to these three questions comprise the basic resume content for any position.

The following list is drawn from the requirements listed in Figure 2.3.

Qualifications for Records Management Officer

REQUIRED	DESIRED
1. Knowledge of filing, retention, and microfilm systems	1. Supervisory experience
2. Ability to write procedures	2. Association or industrial organizational experience
3. College preparation	
4. Three years experience in records management, or equivalent education	

The items in the first column are critical; they must be covered in the resume. The items in the "desired" column are not as rigidly required. If you lack items from the second list, alternatives may be substituted in the resume. (The alternatives may also be discussed in your letter of application.)

FIGURE 2.2. A resume outline organized into general information blocks.

   I. <u>Heading</u>. Required information: name, address (including zip code), and
            telephone number (including area code). Optional information:
            target job title, occupational classification, salary range.

  II. <u>Personal Data</u>. Required information: social security number, date and
            place of birth, and dependents. Optional information:
            height, weight, age, draft status, health, sex, marital
            status, race, and religious preference. (Traditionally this
            block has been placed under the heading as shown, but there
            is now a trend to move it to the end of the resume just
            before references. The choice is up to you.)

 III. <u>Education</u>. Required information most recent first: date of high school
            graduation, graduate and undergraduate degrees, professional
            or correspondence courses, special military training (if appli-
            cable), seminars, scholarships, scholastic honors, internships,
            seminars or academic honors. Provide names and locations of
            all educational institutions and dates for all degrees.

  IV. <u>Experience</u>. Required information most recent first: previous employment
            positions held, job titles, dates of employment, and names of
            organizations. Optional information: highest salary, names
            and addresses of supervisors, description of duties and respon-
            sibilities. (This information may appear before the education
            block if appropriate.)

   V. <u>Military</u>. Required information (if you have military experience):
            branch of service, muster dates, rank, MOS (Military Occupa-
            tion Specialty). Optional information: duties, honors, and
            awards.

  VI. <u>Related Activities</u>. Miscellaneous information that supports the appli-
            cation. (See the discussion to follow.)

 VII. <u>References</u>. Names and addresses of those persons who will vouch for
            the applicant's professional competence, character, or poten-
            tial. (This entire block is optional, but is usually in-
            cluded.)

FIGURE 2.3. A sample job description.

<u>NOTICE OF VACANCY</u>

<u>RECORDS MANAGEMENT OFFICER</u>

General

The National Retired Federal Employees Association and the United States Association of Retired Persons (NRFEA-USARP) are jointly administered, non-profit associations with National Headquarters in Washington, D.C. The purpose of the Associations is to serve retired people and improve their quality of life.

Duties and Responsibilities

Establish and maintain a comprehensive records management program.
Supervise a small clerical staff of approximately twelve people.
Develop an effective central filing system for both groups.
Implement forms control and office manual control programs.
Prepare detailed records analyses, and record retention schedules.

Minimum Requirements

Minimum three years experience in the field of records management, or equivalent education.
Working knowledge of filing, retention, and microfilm systems.
Ability to prepare written procedures.
Previous supervisory experience desired.
College training and experience in forms control.
Association or industrial organizational experience preferred.

Salary Range and Other Information

Starting salary $13,000-17,000, commensurate with qualifications, education, and experience.
Payment of relocation expenses to Washington, D.C. area will be assumed by NRFEA-USARP.
We offer a comprehensive benefits program and ideal working conditions in our new National Headquarters Office building.

Application Procedures

Interested candidates for the position of RECORDS MANAGEMENT OFFICER may send their personal resume, including salary history and other pertinent information to:

Roberta L. Holders
Personnel Specialist
NRFEA-USARP
2020 L Street, NW
Washington, D.C. 20049

WE ARE AN EQUAL OPPORTUNITY EMPLOYER

Besides aiding you in resume preparation, this list will help you decide which jobs you are qualified to pursue. Obviously, if you do not have the minimum specified requirements for a position, you should not apply. But if only one or two of the items in the desired column are missing, do not discard the lead immediately. Use this rule of thumb in deciding whether to apply: If you do not have all of the "requireds," do *not* apply; if you only lack a few of the "desired" qualifications, prepare your resume and apply with confidence.

When employers prepare job descriptions, they often leave room for negotiation. If you have supplementary skills or experience which would allow you to perform a job as well as someone who matches the job description perfectly, take this opportunity to describe them in detail. Use your resume to convince the management that you can do the job. The list of requirements you made from the job description will guide you in constructing your information blocks. Provide information for each item on both lists, substituting alternates for "desired" items you do not have.

Figure 2.4 illustrates a poor, an improved, and a well-constructed information block, using the "experience" category as an example. (The qualifications on the list you compiled will probably fall into either the "experience" or "education" block.) The first example in the figure is entirely inadequate. It is vague and incomplete, and actually raises more questions in the mind of the reader than it answers. If the remainder of the resume were this poorly written, the applicant would almost certainly be rejected. The second version of the same information is more specific; at least it gives the full names of the companies and complete job titles. The final example is the best of all, since it abstracts the applicant's experience in terms of qualifications that are applicable to other positions. This block is more than a list of where the individual had been employed. It is a projection of a positive image. The person described comes across as conscientious, professional, and willing to accept responsibility. Note also that the chronological order in this final block has been reversed to show the most recent experience first. A prospective employer is bound to be most interested in the applicant's present activity; the block should be constructed in this way to correspond with the reader's priorities.

Detailed instruction as to the preparation of each data block is provided later in this chapter. Here it is sufficient to note that a well-written block requires planning and effort. The applicant must determine which information the employer is interested in and present it as briefly and completely as possible. Above all, remember that composing your resume is a process of selection. You need not include everything you have done in your life. The resume is a fact sheet that will supplement other elements of the application process. The physical length and the actual amount of information is not as important to an employer as the relevance of the information to the specific job at hand. In fact, human nature being what it is, a lengthy and detailed resume will probably not be read as thoroughly as a concise one. A survey conducted a few years ago by Harold D. Janes (see Appendix A) showed that most personnel managers prefer resumes to be less than two pages long. This is not a binding rule. You may decide to go beyond this suggested limit, but only if you judge the added information to be significant. Learn to prune and polish.

VISUAL ASPECTS

When a reader looks at a resume for the first time, even before reading it he or she has an unconscious tendency to form an opinion. Usually this impression is crystallized in the first tenth of a second. Even without realizing it readers often ask themselves, Does this resume look

23

FIGURE 2.4. Sample information blocks showing work experience

POOR

1965-1967   Burnwright Industries, Scranton. Clerk.

1967-1970   Keaton

1973   Insurance Underwriters Corporation, Phoenix

1971   Part-time Insurance Sales

IMPROVED

1965-1967   Burnwright Industries, Scranton, PA.
                 Shipping Clerk.

1967-1970   Keaton and Williams Central Insurance Agency,
                 Albuquerque, NM. Salesman.

1970-1972   U.S. Army Active Reserve Duty. Fort Leonard
                 Wood, MO. Lieutenant.

1973-1972   Jefferson Insurance Sales. Part-time Mail
                 Order Insurance Salesman.

1973-present   Insurance Underwriter Corporation of America.
                 Department Supervisor.

GOOD

1973-present   DEPARTMENT SUPERVISOR (New Accounts)
                 Insurance Underwriter Corporation of America,
                 Dubuque, IA. Responsible for office staff of 16.

1973-1972   OWNER: MAIL ORDER INSURANCE COMPANY
                 Affiliated with Jefferson Insurance Sales,
                 New York, NY. Handled 70 accounts while going to college.

1970-1972   LIEUTENANT, U.S. ARMY RESERVE
                 Writer for Solicitor General's Office,
                 Fort Leonard Wood, MO.

1967-1970   SALES COORDINATOR,
                 Keaton and Williams Central Insurance Agency,
                 Albuquerque, NM. Responsible for qualifying direct sales
                 leads for 20 salesmen.

1965-1967   SHIPPING CLERK,
                 Burnwright Industries,
                 Scranton, PA. Responsible for international delivery of
                 corrosive chemicals.

all right? Did the applicant prepare it carefully? Naturally the content of the resume itself will have the greatest effect on an employment decision. But why risk hampering the process with an unappealing application?

The first item that influences the "look" of a resume—though the last to be executed—is the quality of the preparation. The most complex layout in the world won't save a dirty or badly typed resume. Has the applicant taken the time and care necessary to type a clean, errorless copy of the resume? Is it on a high-quality bond paper? Is the type sharp and dark? Mentioning such fundamental items here may seem superfluous, but many employers report that they receive all too many smudged and sloppy applications. If you don't trust your own skill in this area, consider hiring a professional typist to prepare your final draft.

You should attend to some basic principles of graphic design in making your layout decisions. Putting together a stong resume requires a feeling for arrangement, organization, and balance. Think about how the items you wish to present will look on the finished page. Take the time to consider how margins, headings, capital letters, spacing, and underlining can be used to give a sense of orderliness and emphasis to the final resume. You may have to retype your resume a number of times to find out what looks best. Using scissors, tape, and even graph paper, experiment with various layouts and techniques until you discover what pleases you and gives the most effective emphasis to the information you wish to present.

When deciding on what you wish the reader to notice remember that placement equals emphasis. Note as you read the examples throughout this chapter that your attention is drawn to an item when it is stressed graphically. Even the position an item holds on the page has meaning because resumes, and information blocks too, conform to a principle of descending order: Significant items precede those of lesser importance. Therefore, if you feel, for instance, that your experience is more impressive than your education with respect to a certain position, place the experience block above the education block. Your option to select refers to which mode of presentation to use as well as which data to include.

Remember that headings, subheadings, and other items may be placed toward the left-hand margin or centered, and may be typed in all caps or underlined for emphasis. Use indentions and space to set off or add visual emphasis to important points. Make sure too that the information is carefully balanced in the page, both vertically and horizontally.

A simple border line inscribed around the body of your resume can add significantly to the overall appearance. The advantage of this technique is its strong initial appeal; it will make your resume stand out in a stack of others. Draw the final lines with a good quality black pen; the ideal combination is India ink and a drafting pen. If you cannot trust yourself to draw the lines neatly, ask someone you trust to draw them or forget about them altogether. It is better to forgo the border than to send out a resume surrounded by sloppy lines. See Figures 2.5 and 2.6 for examples of the graphic techniques used in resume preparation.

For resumes that extend beyond a single sheet of paper, sequential page numbering should begin with page 2; it is not necessary to number page 1. These numbers may appear in either the upper corner or centered at the top of the sheet. It is also advisable to place some form of specific identification at the top of each sheet. For example:

FIGURE 2.5. A resume demonstrating graphic techniques.

Personal Data Sheet
of Harold Renard
801 Plainfield Avenue, Plainfield, NJ 07060
(102) 882-5544

Applicant for Position of Industrial Engineer

Education

Rensselaer Polytechnic Institute, Troy, NY. 1972-1974. Will
    graduate in Industrial Engineering in June, 1976 (B.S.)
New York Community College, 1968-1970 (A.A.)
Plainfield High School—graduated in 1967

Significant Facts in University Record

Scholastic average of 2.3 grade points at end of 3.5 years
    (2.0 is B)
Area of special interest—water quality control
Student membership in American Institute of Industrial
    Engineers
College Debate Team—1968

Experience

Draftsman, Facilities Design Corporation, Troy, NY (1973-74)
Draftsman, U.S. Army—Service School Qualification (1971-72)
Chainman, Robin Edwards Surveyors, Plainfield, NJ (1968)

Personal Information

Age:	26	Sex:	Male
Place of Birth:	Rouen, France	Health:	Excellent
Citizenship:	U.S.A.	Marital Status:	Single
	Naturalized	Social Security No.:	899-03-044
	(1954)	Military Service:	U.S. Army
			Honorable
			Discharge
			(1972)

References

Mr. Al Bell   Mr. Albert Fredrick
Foreman   Owner
Edwards Surveyors   Facilities Design Corp.
Plainfield, NJ 07063   Troy, NY 12182

Dr. Joel Chandler
Professor of Industrial
    Engineering
Rensselaer Institute
Troy, NY 12180

FIGURE 2.6. Another resume demonstrating graphic techniques.

Resume of:

Marc Moriconi
607 Bridge Street
Wichita Falls, TX 76304

Availability Date:
March 4, 1976

Telephone:
(817) 707-3579

JOB OBJECTIVE

To work as computer operator with hopes of advancing to an upper level management position such as Director of Data Systems.

MILITARY EXPERIENCE

Entered U.S. Army: January 29, 1971   Discharge Date: January 28, 1974

Date: July 1971-October 1973   Missile Repair Parts Specialist
Perform and advise on the use, interchangeability and identification of repair parts for missile material. Maintain Prescribed Loadlist (PPL) for missile units. During this same period was employed as a keypunch operator and worked on the NCR 500.

CIVILIAN EDUCATION

Dates: Graduated June 1969   Central High School, Cape Giraideau, MO.

Dates: 1969-1970   Southeast Missouri State College Cape Giraideau, MO.
Attended 1 year.

Dates: 1972-1973   University of Maryland—European Division. 6 semester hours.

MILITARY EDUCATION

Dates: April 1971-June 1971   Fort Lee, VA
Missile Repair Division
Warehouse Specialist
12 weeks

Dates: October 1973-January 1974   Fort Ord, CA
Computer Operations—thru Project Transition Program. Worked on the IBM 360/40 Computer System. Worked with Multiple Fixed number of Tasks. Duties were the operations of the computer, maintenance of MA 1 2405 tape drives and keypunching.

PERSONAL DATA

Date of Birth: July 8, 1952
Height: 5'10"
Marital Status: Single

Weight: 161
SSN: 556-44-9593
Health: Excellent
No Physical Limitations

References available on request.

```
┌─────────────────────────────────────────────────────────────────────────┐
│                                                                         │
│   Albert Hertz—Resume                                         page 2    │
│                                                                         │
│                              or                                         │
│                                                                         │
│   Page 2                                                    A. L. Hertz  │
│                                                                         │
└─────────────────────────────────────────────────────────────────────────┘
```

Normally, resumes are stapled together to prevent sheets from becoming separated. As an added precaution, though, you may identify each page as to its exact position within the entire package. For example:

```
┌─────────────────────────────────────────────────────────────────────────┐
│                                                                         │
│                                                                         │
│   Albert Hertz—Resume                                      Page 2 of 3  │
│                                                                         │
│                                                                         │
└─────────────────────────────────────────────────────────────────────────┘
```

One final point about resume preparation can be cited as a general rule: Stay away from gimmicks. The "clever" or "cute" resume is very often misunderstood; it tends to convey the impression that the applicant is not a serious person. The exception to this warning is a job situation in which creative abilities are sought and appreciated.

PREPARING INFORMATION BLOCKS

What follows is a detailed consideration of the kinds of data called for by the various information blocks that might be included in a resume. You will notice that some of the data is listed as "optional." Optional information may be included or deleted according to the writer's preference; it may also, under some circumstances, be shifted from one block to another. If, after reading a given section, you are still not sure whether to include an item, your resume will probably be stronger if you simply leave it out.

THE HEADING

The one element common to all resumes regardless of format is the heading. This short block always goes at the top of the first page for identification and reference. The heading should include your name, address, and telephone number, as well as a business number when necessary where you can be reached during the day. It may also include the occupational classification or specific job title you are seeking and the salary you desire.

Title

Titling your resume is optional. If you decide to do so, keep the title brief. Use a single word, "Vita" or "Resume," or a phrase, "Personal Resume of _____ " or "Facts Concerning the Career of _____ ."

If additional pages are required, number them consecutively and mark them with your name in the upper left- or right-hand corner.

Name

Your full and legal name should be the first element following the title. HINT: Type your name in all capital letters to make it more prominent.

Married women may wish to include their maiden names; this is optional.

Avoid nicknames.

Address

A complete and current address including zip code, should follow your name. If your current address is temporary say so and give an alternative if you can. (Be sure to notify the post office when you have a permanent address so your mail will be forwarded without delay.)

If you plan to be traveling when your resume is being considered, arrange to have your mail forwarded or include an itinerary with your resume (on a separate sheet) showing addresses of where you will be at specific times.

Telephone Number

A prospective employer may want to contact you by telephone. Include a number where you can be reached. If the number you give is not your own, explain the circumstances and note the best time of day for contacting you personally.

If no one is available to take a message for you during the day, either include an alternate number of note a time when you will call. If you are in the process of relocating at this time, notify the telephone company of your new number as soon as you have one so they can refer your calls directly.

Do not give the telephone number of your current employer without first obtaining permission.

Always include the correct area code with every phone number.

Position Sought

You may include the occupation classification or title of the position you are seeking in the heading of the resume. You might even wish to elaborate here with a *brief* description of your qualifications.

If you are qualified for more than one position, list them in order of your preference.

Do not write "open" or "anything" here. A personnel officer might not take the time to discover what you are best suited for and could just file your application away.

NOTE: Including the position sought is optional *unless* you are not planning to send a cover letter—that is, a letter of application to introduce yourself.

Desired Salary

Optional. If you choose to mention the salary you desire in your resume (see the discussion of salary in Chapters 3 and 4 before you decide), keep your demand flexible at this stage. Either refer to an acceptable salary range, cite your last salary, or simply state that the question is "negotiable."

Photograph

A photograph is optional in a resume; by law, an employer cannot require you to provide one prior to hiring. Ask yourself if such an inclusion will increase your chance of getting the position you are applying for. Remember that photographs are expensive, particularly if you send out a number of resumes.

Never include a photograph that is unflattering or out of date.

Goals

A statement of your professional plans and goals is of particular importance if you are just beginning your career. Such a statement is optional, but if you decide against including it in your resume, you should incorporate it in your letter of application or personal interview plan.

NOTE: In a recent survey, a majority of personnel recruiters from industry clearly indicated that they were particularly interested in this item when interviewing recent college graduates.

THE PERSONAL-DATA BLOCK

The personal-data section of the resume contains your vital statistics, the most specific information about you. Include only those points you feel are relevant to your employment history and might be of interest to an employer. The list that follows is composed of all *possible* items, but they would probably never appear in the same resume. A brief personal-data block, for instance, might only include your social security number, date of birth, and the number of dependents you wish to declare—all necessary as tax information. A more extensive block could include height, weight, and health data; on the other hand, you might decide to provide no personal information at all.

You also have a choice as to where to place your personal-data block. Traditionally, personal information went at the top of the first page and formed part of the heading. Recently, though, applicants have tended to de-emphasize personal information, choosing to stress experience, education, and training as the significant factors in job selection. Thus the personal-data block is showing up more frequently at the end of the resume immediately above the references. The choice in this matter is purely subjective.

Social Security Number

Optional. This number is required by an employer at the time of hiring for tax accounting purposes. Also, in larger organizations your social security number may be used as an employee identification number. But it is not required on a resume.

Height and Weight

Optional. Including this information is a dying custom.

There is no real reason to do so except to give the reader a general physical impression of the applicant—rarely a factor in hiring.

30

Age

Optional. Before volunteering your age in your resume, ask yourself if it could be considered a negative factor for a particular position. Treat such information as optional at this early stage.

Date of Birth

Optional. At the time of hiring, many companies require this information for insurance and retirement purposes. In the resume, though, you can treat it as optional. If you do include the date of birth, provide the month, day, and year. Avoid using military dating (day-month-year) in civilian situations.

Place of Birth

Optional for American citizens. If you do include it show city or town and state; county is not necessary. If you wish to state that you are a citizen, use "United States citizen" rather than "American citizen."

If you were born in another country, include a statement of your present legal situation. Clarify visa, citizenship, or nationalization status. Be sure this information is current and complete.

Health

A normal health record is usually noted as "good" or "excellent"—never "perfect."

If you do have a physical problem or disability that does not affect your employment potential but which you wish to mention, you may direct the reader to "see attachment." A detailed explanation of the situation, with any requisite medical endorsements, can then be appended to the resume. This technique may also be used if the applicant has a criminal record, or any other sensitive item that an employer might consider negative unless provided with an explanation.

Military History

Required. Dates of entry and discharge, branch of service, rank, and type of discharge are appropriate here. Since the government and many employers give preference to veterans, do not overlook this opportunity to mention your military record.

If your military background is extensive or particularly noteworthy—for example, if you are a retired service person—you may wish to emphasize it even more by placing it, in detail, in a special resume block.

Military Status

Since the abolition of the Selective Service, this information is not as crucial to a potential employer as it was in the past. But if you have a current military reserve or national guard obligation that could affect your working hours or vacation time, mention it here.

Dependents

Optional. A declaration of the number of persons being supported entirely by your income, or a statement of the number of exemptions you wish to declare, is a tax-related question that will be required when you are hired. You may expand on this information by including the names of your immediate family or information about your spouse, such as education or career. Such information adds a personal touch.

Sex

A "male" or "female" label is optional. You may wish to include it, though, if your name could lead to confusion—for example, if your name is Leslie, or if you sign yourself J. D. Withers.

Race and Religious Preference

Optional. This information is covered by the Fair Labor Practices Code. An employer cannot require you to include it, but with regard to the current emphasis on affirmative action, you may wish to volunteer it if you are a member of a minority.

Special Credentials

Required, if applicable. This section should include any special licenses, certificates, ratings or clearances that may be required for employment, such as a current real estate broker's license or a military clearance. If your credentials are of particular significance, you may wish to emphasize them further by placing them in a separate block of their own.

Credentials that are not mandatory for a particular position should be included in the related-activities block.

Finances

Statements concerning your personal finances are optional. However, if your economic situation is exceptionally stable, or you own real estate or any other capital investments, you may feel that these facts favorably reflect your job-related skills and choose to mention them briefly here.

Another item of interest to many employers is the recent graduate's degree of self-support while attending college. This information is optional, but can be mentioned here or as a separate item later in the body of the resume.

Residence

Owning one's own home is often a factor in an applicant's willingness to relocate. Naturally this information would be considered if the desired position involved relocation.

THE EDUCATION BLOCK

An applicant's academic record is one of two basic considerations in job screening. A personnel officer determines whether an applicant is "qualified" and should be interviewed by weighing schooling or other special training against experience gained through employment.

Naturally, the importance of your formal education is directly related to the job under consideration, and the emphasis that you give it on your resume will depend on your analysis of the job description. Many positions have "minimum educational requirements." But some descriptions state that a certain educational level is "preferred." In such a case, if you do not meet the preferred level you are invited to show that your experience or special training make you a qualified applicant.

In its most abbreviated form, the education block is a list, with dates, of the schools you attended—in reverse chronological order beginning with the most recent first—and the degrees or certificates you received. Personnel directors, however, often suggest that this information be expanded to include a summary of the course work completed or an explanation of nature of specialized training. Follow this rule of thumb: If your record speaks for itself, keep it brief. But if education is important in obtaining a certain position, and you feel that your record is not strong enough or does not obviously apply, then emphasize in detail what you have. In Figure 2.5 above, for example, Harold Renard strengthened his education block by adding the subsection "Significant Facts in University Record."

Remember that the amount and nature of detailed information required will depend on the job objective you have in mind. If you have a B.S. degree in data processing and are looking for a position in the field, a complete list of your major courses and computer languages would be appropriate in your education block. On the other hand, if, with the same degree, you are seeking a job as a retail sales manager, a brief statement of the degree field and a detailed list of elective courses in business management would be more appropriate.

Applicants often wonder if they should include grades on a resume. If your grades are good, then by all means use them as an asset. If your grades are average or poor avoid mentioning them; simply state that you completed a given program.

A "B" average or better is above the norm; include it in its finest light by computing the most favorable grade point average, or G.P.A. For example, you might have received mediocre grades during the first two years of college, then changed your major and became an excellent student. In this case, a four-year, cumulative average of grades would not give an accurate picture of your academic ability or accomplishments in your field. You should compute your G.P.A. from your grades during the last two years, or only from the courses you took in your new major. Notice how the same data can be computed in significantly different ways:

	Grade Point Average
Overall (all four years)	2.63
Upper Division (last two years)	3.01
Upper Division Courses in Major	3.31
Senior Level Courses in Major	3.40

Needless to say, you will want to cite the figure that shows you to the best advantage, particularly with respect to your specialty.

Round out your education block by listing any scholastic awards, special acknowledgments, or honors you might have received and any professional organizations you might have belonged to. Graduates of schools or colleges which did not use conventional grading systems can convey some idea of their academic achievement by providing a detailed account of these honors and organiza-

33

tions. Or they may submit personal letters of recommendation from faculty members along with their application packages.

Seniors in college often prepare and send out resumes before they have graduated. These applicants should give the month and year they began the degree program and note the progress they have made to date, ending the entry with the words "will graduate" and the estimated date. Students in advanced programs who are uncertain as to whether they will complete them might decide not to mention the degree at all. They could refer to any courses already completed as "additional work for professional growth," or "academic specialization beyond the Baccalaureate."

THE EXPERIENCE BLOCK

One frequently decides which job to apply for on the basis of past employment. Some, if not all, of your past experience could have made you into a valuable asset to other organizations. Therefore, in preparing the employment block for your resume, exercise your option to review your past and decide where to place the emphasis. At hiring some companies and government agencies may require a complete record of the positions you have held, but in your resume you need only include that experience which relates to the present job description.

Again, list your past employment experiences in reverse chronological order, with your most recent job first. Include the name of the employer and the position you held. If you wish to emphasize certain jobs, give the specific job titles, a brief description of your responsibilities, and your highest salaries. Be consistent and include the same information for all items listed.

Keep in mind that you are preparing this list for someone else to read. Do not assume that what is obvious to you will also be obvious to another. Consider the overall impression that this section will leave with a prospective employer who has not met you personally. Stress your strong points. For example, if you have a long history of professional positions in a single field, a simple list may suffice. You might want to describe the most significant experience; in this case, the label is "Sample Description." If your list of jobs becomes too cumbersome, consider titling the block "Representative Experience," taking care to note that the list has been condensed for convenience. On the other hand, if you have recently graduated from high school or college, you may have very little hard data to include in your experience block. In this case, you could decide to describe each job you did have more fully. For example:

Service-Station Attendant	Responsible for opening and closing, posting daily accounts, and maintaining inventory.
Retail Sales Clerk	Face-to-face experience with the public. Familiar with order and receipt forms, inventory control, and handling money. Bonded.

The key to this method is to abstract from an otherwise unimpressive job the experience that is applicable to more responsible positions.

Some job titles are so vague that a detailed description is called for—for example, District Sales Manager or Administrative Assistant. Take this opportunity to demonstrate that your background has prepared you for a leadership appointment. The objective in this block is to show that your preparation coincides with the employer's concept of a "good" candidate for the job. Use the language in the job description to present your qualifications. Look over the sample job descriptions in Chapter 1 to see how different companies explain what type of person they are looking for.

If the job you are applying for requires a great deal of past experience, you may decide to place this information ahead of the education block. In some cases, when formal education is irrelevant and your experience very impressive you can delete the education block entirely. Any items that are placed toward the beginning of the resume will automatically have greater impact on the reader. In Figure 2.7, for instance, job experience and management orientation are emphasized; this information is discussed in detail before education is touched upon.

In summary, try to focus your experience whenever possible. Study job descriptions in your field of interest and see what qualities they have in common. Then list these key words to use as guides when describing your past experience. Do most positions seem to be seeking persons who can accept responsibility? have management experience? work well with other people? Compare your background with each of these qualities until you determine which factors you should emphasize or expand in your resume. Equally important, decide what is not important and delete.

If you have difficulty identifying qualities in your own experience that employers tend to look for, try making a list of the tasks your past employment required you to do. Then simply look for the factors that they have in common and emphasize them as major qualifications. In the Figure 2.8, a stenographer's skills and duties are itemized and "responsibility" is seen to be the common thread running through them all. Diversity or conscientiousness might also be abstracted from this list as well. Can you find other qualities the items have in common?

THE MILITARY BLOCK

All former military personnel should mention their service in the resume. As noted earlier, many employers, for example the Civil Service Commission, give preferred consideration to former military personnel when hiring. You need not make a separate block, however. If you can sum up your service in a line or two, enter this information in the personal-data or related-activities block. If, however, one of the following conditions applies to you, describe your service in a separate block:

1. You have had specific training or experience which has prepared you for a specific civilian job.

2. Military service makes up a large portion of your background.

Again, this information should be listed in reverse chronological order, with your most recent experience first. This block should include branch of service, dates of entry and discharge, rank, and military occupation specialty. You may also describe your duties and cite promotions, proficiency certificates, ratings, commendations, and awards. If this information is extensive, subdivide the section for convenience.

If you feel it would be advantageous to describe any portion of your service experience or responsibilities in detail, handle the information as explained in the preceding section, relating

35

FIGURE 2.7. A sample resume emphasizing the applicant's experience.

Robert M. Uchimura
73 S. Locust St.
Rowland Heights, CA 91748
(213) 964-8090

GENERAL QUALIFICATIONS

Marketing and Business Planning
Program Management and Control
Financial Planning Management
Proposal Preparation and Management

MARKETING AND BUSINESS PLANNING

Developed, monitored, and controlled product line/business plans for a major division of a medium-sized company. Detailed business plans are prepared each year and monitored, controlled, and updated each month. Top level five-year business plans are also prepared each year. Plans included market analysis, sales forecast, sales strategy and tactics, expected profit margins, and resource requirements.

PROGRAM MANAGEMENT AND CONTROL

Managed R&D programs ranging in value from $20,000 to $2,000,000, varying from two months to eighteen months duration, concerned with development of data processing and sensor systems. Performed program scheduling, cost estimating, and control of these programs.

FINANCIAL PLANNING AND MANAGEMENT

Responsible for recommending allocation of company discretionary resources (Bid & Proposal and IR&D funds) to top management. Monitored, controlled, and periodically re-allocated funds as required. Also monitored capital expenditures necessary to satisfy marketing objectives. Performed ROI analysis for each business area from historical and forecasted sales to determine allocation of resources.

PROPOSAL PREPARATION AND MANAGEMENT

Involved in writing, organization, and direction of proposals for development of advanced data processing systems and sensor systems.

EDUCATION

M.B.A.	Business Administration	1971
M.S.	Electrical Engineering	1967
B.S.	Electrical Engineering	1964
B.S.	Mathematics	1963

FIRMS

1971-1974	Market Planning: ElectroSystems, Azusa, CA
1964-1971	Project Engineering: Ryan Aircraft, Fullerton, CA

PERSONAL

Birth date: June 3, 1942

SECURITY CLEARANCE: Secret   References are on file.

FIGURE 2.8. Identifying a common characteristic in a list of duties.

```
Stenographer's Duties:

Schedules
Appointments
Correspondence
Shorthand            } = RESPONSIBILITY
Reception
Security Clearance
Bonded/Notary
```

your duties and responsibilities to the job for which you are applying. Use civilian terminology
whenever possible.

The Related Skills and Activities Block

The block dealing with "related skills and activities," set toward the end of the resume,
allows you the greatest freedom in selection and therefore the greatest opportunity for individu-
alizing your resume. In this section provide any information that may indirectly reinforce your
professional qualifications and give a prospective employer a clearer picture of you as a person
and as a professional. Also include here those facts which you chose not to include in other
blocks but which you do not wish to delete entirely.

Since this section is composed of miscellaneous material, the form of presentation is up to
you. You may present the data in an itemized listing under a single heading, or, for convenience
and emphasis, subdivided under separate headings, such as special education, professional, military, community services, personal data, and so forth.

Any information in this block is optional; so you can select anything which you feel adds to
previous points or balances the thrust of the resume. For instance, you may feel that the educational and employment data previously presented, though adequate, gave too narrow an impression of
you as a person. In the related-activities block you could broaden the picture by referring to
activities that show your strong interest in community affairs or volunteer work. Or, if you are
interested in a management position, you may reinforce this preference by listing offices you hold
or have held in various clubs and organizations. However, you may simply wish to compile items to
show that you have a generalized background in a number of areas. Such information should be
selected with reference both to the composite professional portrait you wish to project and to the
job for which you are applying. Keep in mind that an employer is looking for a capable person—
plus!

Examples of related-activities items are listed below. Browse through these lists; use them
to jog your memory. But remember, these are *sample* lists and not all-inclusive.

Education-Related Activities: Membership or offices held in organizations or clubs, civic
groups, involvement in student government, academic honors or awards, athletic participation,

37

assistantships, scholarships, grade point average, standing in graduating class, forensics, journalism or theater experience, ROTC, conventions or meetings attended, letters of achievement or commendation, publications, alumni activities, and so forth.

Professional Activities: Conferences or meetings attended, special schooling or training, publications, speaking engagements, seminars, patents, awards and recognitions, sales records, supervisory experience, commendations, memberships in professional organizations or associations, internships, advanced courses of study, travel, teaching experience, areas of expertise or special qualifications, ratings, licenses, certificates, and so forth.

Service Activities: Civic projects, volunteer work, welfare work, church or political activities, awards, honors or commendations, memberships, offices held in clubs or organizations, supervisory positions, special interests, and so forth.

Military Activities: See detailed discussion in previous section.

Special Skills: Languages spoken or read; office-machine proficiency and speed; typing or shorthand speed; stenotype; computer languages; first aid; lifesaving; equipment ratings; various driving, flying and radio licenses; special certificates; ratings or licenses that show proficiencies; and so forth.

Some applicants may wish to include a category of non-job-related personal activities, such as hobbies or special interests, in the resume. Two schools of thought prevail on the advisability of including such information. Those who wish to further the "well-rounded" image feel that such information is desirable. But those who favor avoiding clichés at all costs take this position: "If all you can find to add is 'skiing, stamp collecting, and a desire to work with other people, why include it?" On this point you are well-advised to review the overall thrust of the resume and decide if your personal interests are relevant. For example, an applicant's past experience in social organizations and inclination for travel would be desirable qualities for a sales-related position in a nationwide company. But, unless the specific job description calls for this type of background, it is a good idea to leave strictly personal and irrelevant material out of the resume.

The easiest way to compile information for inclusion in the related-activities block is to list *all* your experience and skills and then go back and delete the weakest points. Learning to leave out extraneous information is the key to preparing a well-focused and direct resume. Ask yourself at every point, "Is this information relevant? Why?" If you have any doubt about a point, leave it out. Avoid padding. Long lists of inappropriate and unrelated data are boring to read and tend to detract from the important points. When you do decide to include a point, avoid distorting the information to make it and you appear more attractive. Don't *ever* risk a "white lie" at any stage of the job-search process. Aim for a balance that is straightforward and modest.

REFERENCES AND LETTERS OF RECOMMENDATION

An applicant should be able to offer an employer the names of individuals who will vouch for his or her professional competence, character, or potential in the chosen field. Usually, a list of three to five names and addresses (titles and telephone numbers are optional) of people you know are willing to speak for you appears on the resume. However, you may choose to provide references separately, particularly if you are sending out many resumes and wish to protect your references from being inundated with calls. In this case a notation, such as "references available on request" or "references are on file," is appropriate. Whichever method you choose always include on the resume the offer to make references available.

When you are preparing a list of references for a general-employment situation where diversity is an asset, try to include persons who have known you in different situations so they may speak about various qualities. The combined descriptions could result in a broader and more accurate picture of you as a person. But if you are applying for a specific position, choose references who can emphasize the specialized nature of your skills or personality. For example, a college graduate applying for an assistantship would be wise to choose as references past college professors exclusively; they will understand the applicant's needs *and* the expectations of readers.

As a courtesy, contact the people you wish to include on your reference list and ask for permission to use their names. (See Figure 2.9 for a sample letter of request.) This contact will allow them to prepare adequate answers to questions about you so they will not be caught by surprise when prospective employers call. Also, they can take this opportunity to decline permission. A refusal could be a blessing in disguise; it could protect you against the possibility of someday discovering a "bad" recommendation in your personnel files. (A potential employer is not likely to tell you if a reference gave you a poor report.) Finally, it may be worthwhile to reintroduce yourself to the people on your list, particularly if you have not spoken to them for a while.

Some prospective employers are satisfied with a list of persons they can contact for references. Others require letters of recommendation. Employers' preference aside, you may decide that you wish to collect a series of letters to show upon request. In either case, you are responsible for seeing that the people writing letters of recommendation have sufficient information about you and the position you are seeking to supplement your application with strong support data. Their individual responses can then be used to reinforce the major elements of your application and resume. Use the following step-by-step approach to insure that your references can provide relevant information, especially if you have not contacted them recently. This approach is based on a personal-interview technique, but a letter of request (see Figure 2.9) or a telephone call will work as well if a personal meeting is impractical.

A Reference-Interview Checklist

1. Contact the individuals and ask them if they will write a letter of recommendation for you.

2. Arrange a meeting, at their convenience, to discuss the recommendation.

3. Bring the following items to the meeting, and leave them for reference when composing the letter of recommendation:

    a. A copy of your most current resume, and letter of application, if you have prepared one.

    b. A description of the job you are seeking, and some information about the nature of the company.

    c. A brief list of the situations in which the two of you worked together. The person writing the letter of recommendation may find it useful to cite these specific occasions.

FIGURE 2.9. A sample letter to a prospective reference.

37 N.W. 37th Street
Gainesville, FL 32601
November 30, 1976

Dr. Wesley Van Nostrand
Chemical Engineering Department
University of Miami
P.O. Drawer 9088
Coral Gables, FL 33124

Dear Dr. Van Nostrand:

During the time that you were my graduate adviser at the university, you expressed an interest in helping me find a position that would allow me to continue my research. At the recent CEAA meeting in New York, Dr. Fred Endfield spoke to me about a position as a research chemist in his division of Chiefow.

Would you kindly send a letter of recommendation to their personnel office for me? The address is:

Personnel Officer
Chiefow Chemicals
125 Lexington Street
Sweet Springs, MO 65351

I am enclosing my resume, a copy of the Chiefow job description, and a description of my most recent project work with Row Specialties, where I have been a field analyst for three years.

If you have any further questions, please call me at my home after 6:00. The number is (305) 378-0848.

Thank you for helping me.

Sincerely,

Robert A. Wise

Robert A. Wise

4. If you intend to use the letter for more than one job, explain your job application program, showing the individuals how you intend to use the letter of recommendation. Don't tell anyone what to write; simply sketch out the most advantageous approach as you see it.

5. Ask the persons for their opinions or advice on how to improve your approach to the application. Make any necessary adjustments and thank them for their assistance.

6. Some time later, send a note of appreciation to each person who writes a letter for you.

You may also include in the reference section of your resume an offer to bring samples of your work to the interview (though you could reserve this offer for your application letter). Naturally, such a suggestion depends on the nature of your field, and the availability of such examples. For example, a graphic artist or a draftsman might offer to show a portfolio of graphic work, a salesman may wish to bring letters of commendation or service awards to an interview, while a teacher could show lesson plans or student evaluations. Decide whether or not you have some easily portable items that would substantiate your professional skill to a prospective employer.

THE PROSE RESUME

For certain positions—usually those requiring executive-type initiative, increased responsibility or decision-making skills—a more detailed discussion of the applicant's background is required from the very beginning of the job-search process. In such cases a "prose resume," which elaborates each point, is preferable to the standard resume, which merely outlines qualifications.

In the following excerpt from a prose resume, an executive secretary's employment record and related experience are described fully in terms of responsibility and results:

Originally hired as general secretary, Class 4. Promoted to private secretary, Class 2. Assigned to the Comptroller's Office because of special skills in personalized letter writing, schedule management, and dictation.

Responsible for screening all incoming correspondence, and answering, when appropriate, in the Comptroller's name. Supervised office staff of two stenographers and one file clerk.

Received three meritory salary increases, two annual service bonuses, and was nominated in the Division for Secretary of the Year.

Notice that the descriptions are written in a series of short phrases, usually beginning with a verb. This style allows the writer to be complete *and* concise. If you choose to use full sentences, your resume will take on the form of a long letter of application.

The prose resume is the most personalized possible resume. Its fundamental advantage is its thoroughness and increased applicability to certain types of positions, usually in management. It is related to the standard resume the way a passage from a book is related to an outline of that passage. The prose resume does have disadvantages, though. It requires more time to prepare as well as to read. There is a chance that it may not be read fully simply because of its length.

Therefore, if an applicant elects to compose a prose resume, it is suggested that a summary or standard resume be submitted as a cover document. This technique is demonstrated in the extended resumes in Figures 2.10 and 2.11. Note that a compromise format is demonstrated in Figure 2.7, cited earlier. In this example, Robert Uchimura prepared a one-page prose resume by simply deleting all extraneous information and focusing on his strongest qualification, experience.

A CHECKLIST FOR RESUME PREPARATION

Use the following list when preparing your own resume.

1. Is the resume appropriate for the job? Is it complete?
2. Is it scrupulously neat—no strike-overs or erasures?
3. Is each item correct and complete? Dates? Numbers? Names?
4. Does the organization of the resume emphasize the points I wish to stress?
5. Is the language appropriate? Have I misspelled any words?
6. Have I left anything out? Does everything have a purpose?
7. Have I contacted the references?
8. Does the resume have a professional look?
9. Is the heading complete and up to date? Can the reader get in touch with me?
10. Will I need a cover letter?

FIGURE 2.10. A sample prose resume.

PERSONAL RESUME

Richard Sanker   Telephone
710 Nostrand Avenue   Home: (516) 554-7817
Hempstead, NY 11553   Work: (212) 381-7007

EMPLOYMENT OBJECTIVE: A position in management team building

PERSONAL DATA   Marital status: Single
                       Date of birth : June 17, 1949
                       Height/Weight : 5' 10'' / 150 lbs.
                       Health   : Excellent

EDUCATION

M.B.A., 1974-1975, Hofstra University, NY
  Field of Concentration—Organizational Development (Behavioral Sciences)
  Grade Point Average—3.9 (4.0 Scale)
  Graduate education financed by Fellowship, Hofstra University
  Extracurricular activities—Graduate Representative, University Goals and
    Planning Committee, Graduate Honor Society

B.S., 1971-1973, Hofstra University, Major—Business Administration/Communi-
    cation
  Grade Point Average—3.3 (4.0 Scale); graduated with honors (Top 10 percent
    of Class)
  Extracurricular activities—Student Dean, Law Department; Course Evaluation
    Committee Vice-president; Biddle Law Society; Faculty Tenure Commission

A.A., 1970-1972, New York Community College, Major—Business Administration
  Grade Point Average—3.0 (4.0 Scale)

MILITARY SERVICE

  1969-1973, Served in New York National Guard, Received Honorable Discharge.

MANAGEMENT EXPERIENCE

October 1974 to present: City of New York, Coordinating Office for Drug and
Alcohol Abuse Programs, responsible to Managing Director and Mayor's Office,
City of New York.
    Position: Training and Organizational Development Specialist
    Responsibilities: Responsible for working with top-level administrators
in the development and implementation of intensive staff development programs.
I acted as an external consultant to 80 various agencies which employed approximately 1000 employees. I was also responsible for all internal staff
development operations. (For specific information, see Supplementary Resume
page 3.)

October 1972 to January 1973: Organizational Renewal Associates, Consultant
to Trenton Central High School, Trenton, New Jersey. Responsibilities:
Conduct series of nine workshops involving skill development, group problem-
solving techniques, Open systems Planning, and group decision-making processes.

June 1972 to September 1972: Hofstra University, Management Development
Laboratory, staff member. Fifty hours experience in direct teaching of
undergraduate course in behavioral science, ten three-hour training sessions
in interpersonal development and group dynamics, and ten two-hour training
sessions in group problem-solving and decision-making skills.

EXPERIENCE IN COMPUTER OPERATIONS

June 1970 to September 1970: Computer Operator, First shift. Shared Medical Systems, Prussia, New York. Responsible for computer operations, IBM system 360 Disc/Tape terminal system.

June 1967 to November 1968: Tabulation and Computer Operations. Jameson Computing and Tabulations Company, Philadelphia, Pennsylvania (presently a subsidiary of Provident National Corporation, Stock Exchange Building, 17th Samson Street, New York). Was responsible for major operations for several large accounts. Also involved in programming.

SUPPLEMENTARY RESUME

Because of the unique nature of my position as Training and Organizational Development Specialist, I feel it is necessary to explain in some detail my responsibilities and accomplishments. The following is a summary of my involvement with the Coordinating Office for Drug and Alcohol Abuse Programs which is directly responsible to the Managing Director and Mayor's Office, City of New York.

Attitude Survey Project: Developed diagnostic-intervention survey to identify organizational strengths and weaknesses. As project director of this survey, was responsible for all four phases of the diagnosis and analysis, development of workshops around strengths and weaknesses, interventions, and an evaluation of effectiveness.

Criminal Justice System Coordination: As project director, was responsible for developing a project to eliminate the duplication of services within the criminal justice system.

Computer Evaluation Study: Was responsible for evaluating manual-operations system for purpose of computerization of patient-accountability system. Served as head of search committee in the selection of computer firms that would fulfill our service requirements.

Management By Objectives (MBO): Researched current materials for use as a diagnostic tool in determining organizational goals and objectives. Study was used in conjunction with the above attitude survey for the purpose of developing a management team-building project.

Open-Systems Planning Project: As project director, was responsible for conducting extensive workshops to clarify organizational objectives. Evaluated and developed a process by which staff members could resolve issues as follows.
   1. Define core processes and core technologies
   2. Identify critical interactions—domains, demands, responses
   3. Cause and effect relationships—using total-systems approach
   4. Increase degree of congruency between domains, demands, and responses
   5. Sociotechnical systems evaluation, to focus around task projects

Management Team-Building: Was responsible for conducting series of workshops around several basic team-building issues—competition, cooperation, interviewing techniques, listening responses, X-Y management theories, problem-solving, decision making, leadership, motivation, and role clarification. Operated and evaluated team-building effectiveness around three basic goals:
   1. To increase commonality and congruence throughout the system around such central issues as goals, roles, rewards, communication, influence, and decision making.
   2. To enlarge the manager's sense of his role to include the needs of the organization as a whole as well as those of his own subsystem.

3. To develop management processes that are more efficient in the use of technical and human resources, and that increase interdependence and collaboration.

The process of team-building focuses on enlarging common awareness to relevant issues, and improving diagnostic and problem-solving technology, group processes and interpersonal skills.

COMMENTS FROM ASSOCIATES:

"I have had the occasion to observe Mr. Sanker both as an employer and as an independent observer after he left my employ. Richard is a very competent technician in the areas of computer programming, financial operations, and as a system analyst. He responds rapidly to new situations and masters new information quickly. In addition to being able to define problems and formulate solutions he is also competent to assist in the implementation of the solutions. In addition to having considerable technical knowledge in a number of areas he also has the ability to get along well with others, both on a management and worker level. He is able to communicate effectively, motivate others and to organize group activities so as to maintain high morale and efficient operations."

V. F. Karlson, Financial Consultant

"Richard Sanker was a student in several of my Information Systems and operations research courses at the Graduate School of Management, Hofstra University, in 1967 and 1968. He also was a programmer-analyst in the Hofstra Emergency Medical Systems Project in 1968 which I managed. I found him to be conscientious, diligent, and competent in his professional area. He was easy to work with and fit easily into project teams. Based on my limited association, I would recommend him as a competent, trained quantitative analyst."

Arthur Y. Randolph, Manager
Systems Planning and Economics Division

"He is intelligent and hard-working and particularly competent in the area of sophisticated investment research. I know him to be a good programmer with experience in a variety of computer systems."

Warren M. Brandt, Regional Manager
National Time Sharing System

"I have always found him to be a very hard-working and dedicated person. He takes his duties and responsibilities seriously and takes great care to see that his projects are completed. The quality I admire most about Richard is his genuine desire to do the very best job possible, under any circumstances."

Audrey V. Renshaw, Supervisor
Performance Reporting

FIGURE 2.11. Another sample prose resume accompanied by a standard resume.

GLORIA CLAIBORNE

4567 S. Bronson Street, Los Angeles, CA 90011

SUMMARY OF EMPLOYMENT EXPERIENCE
(Please see expanded resume for details.)   EMPLOYER

1972-1976   Associate Professor: University of California,
             Sociology & Counseling   Los Angeles, Campus

1971-1972   Administrative Assistant: Office of the Under-Secretary,
             Implemented service de-   Department of Health, Education
             livery systems for states   & Welfare, Washington, D.C.
             of Georgia and Oregon.

1970-1971   Special Assistant: Commissioner of Social &
             Developed departmental   Rehabilitation Services (HEW)
             personnel practices   Washington, D.C.
             and policies.

1968-1970   Rehabilitation Counselor: Watts Service Center,
             Coordinated DVR and HRD   California Department of
             programs.   Vocational Rehabilitation

1966-1968   Group Counceling Specialist: California Department of
             Developed programs in   Vocational Rehabilitation
             minority urban areas.

1966-1965   Rehabilitation Intern: Langley Porter Neuropsychia-
             Established the position.   tric Center, San Francisco

1964-1966   Group Work Supervisor: YMCA, Mission Branch,
             Recruited and trained   San Francisco
             advisors.

1962-1964   Center Director, and   Department of Recreation,
             Head Director: City of Oakland
             Administration of facilities
             and staff.

1956-1961   Recreation Director, and   Department of Recreation,
             Senior Supervising Director: City of Detroit
             Program development.

ADDITIONAL TEACHING EXPERIENCE

   Two years as a part-time member of the graduate faculty, California State
   University, Los Angeles, teaching candidates in psychological and social
   aspects of disability.

EDUCATION

   B.S.   Wayne State University (1961)
   M.S.   California State University, San Francisco (1966)
   Ph.D.   University of Southern California (in progress)

ADDITIONAL EDUCATION

   Langley Porter Neuropsychiatric Institute—Internship (1966).
   Western Behavioral Sciences Institute—Advanced T-Group (1967).

EXPANDED RESUME

GLORIA CLAIBORNE   Administrative Assistant, or
4567 S. Bronson Street   Rehabilitation Counselor in
Los Angeles, CA 90011   Education, Government or
(213) 235-8910   Industry

EVALUATION OF RELEVANT EXPERIENCE

Department of Health, Education,
and Welfare, Washington, D.C., 1971-1972

> DUTIES: Assisted the Commissioner of Social and Rehabilitation Services
> in fundamental policy areas related to personnel of the Department. De-
> veloped and wrote legislation and personnel-practices code, and studied
> new program areas.
>
> Aided the Under-Secretary in implementation of service delivery systems
> to states, counties and urban areas. Collaborated in the design of spe-
> cial systems for the states of Georgia and Oregon.
>
> SUMMARY: Participated in the implementation of ideas into policies on
> the national level. Strengthened my ability to analyze situations and
> make appropriate decisions. Developed my skills in administration in
> large bureaucratic organizations. Increased my knowledge of special
> personnel problems, especially in rehabilitation.

Department of Vocational
Rehabilitation, State of California, 1966-1970

> DUTIES: General rehabilitation counselor to the Watts area of Los
> Angeles, following a period of serious difficulty. Coordinated the DVR
> and HRD program services for clients at the Watts Service Center.
>
> Developed and implemented innovative counseling programs to assist "dis-
> advantaged" clients in the areas of decision making, personal relations,
> and community awareness. Worked extensively in South Central Los
> Angeles, South East Los Angeles, Long Beach and Venice—communities com-
> posed of highly diverse ethnic backgrounds.
>
> SUMMARY: Developed my skills in evaluating the needs of large groups of
> ethnically and racially mixed groups in terms of rehabilitation counsel-
> ing. Allowed me to develop new programs and evaluate their success—
> two of the innovations I introduced have been adopted by the State of
> California.

Langley Porter Neuropsychiatric
Center, San Francisco, 1965-1966

> DUTIES: Established the role of rehabilitation counselor at the insti-
> tute. Worked as counselor with patients in the Day/Night unit. Cooper-
> ated with occupational therapists and hospital volunteer coordinators to
> establish tolerance and work experience program for the patients. Made
> appropriate DVR referrals from among patients, and developed employment-
> preparation programs for job-ready patients. Functioned as therapist
> for the out-patient clinic and family-therapy unit and conducted therapy
> seminars for staff personnel.
>
> SUMMARY: Developed an entire rehabilitation program, from start to
> finish, and evaluated its success in terms of immediate and long-range
> patient needs. Increased my ability to coordinate a program with other

programs in the most effective manner. Increased my personal experience
in administration and budgeting and my basic knowledge of organizational
structures and policy making. Gained invaluable experience too in the
individual needs of patients in counseling areas.

YMCA, Mission Branch,
San Francisco, 1964-1966

DUTIES: Recruited, trained, and supervised volunteer club advisors.
Conducted leadership and vocational training workshops for club officers
and members. Led sensitivity-training groups for staff and members—the
latter was composed primarily of teenage blacks and browns.

SUMMARY: Developed my skills in coordinating a program in community
counseling. Allowed me to work with young people in terms of their
needs—awareness, ego development, and goals—and to combine this with
work being done by the staff.

Department of Recreation,
City of Oakland, 1962-1964

DUTIES: Responsible for administering, supervising and evaluating facilities, staff and programs serving teens, young adults and senior citizens. Coordinated with community through Associated Agencies (a cooperative program of public agencies which included recreation, police,
public health, youth authority, probation, schools, and welfare
services). Also worked closely with the Community Council (the PTAs of
all schools in the area).

SUMMARY: Gave me broad knowledge and experience in the organizing programs that relate to numerous elements of community life. Increased my
skills in implementation of new programs, many of which I designed, to
meet the needs of many types of people.

Department of Recreation,
City of Detroit, 1956-1961

DUTIES: Planned and implemented recreational programs for teens, young
adults, and senior citizens in a racially mixed community center. Supervised part-time staff, wrote progress and evaluation reports, and
coordinated efforts with related public agencies.

Developed program for handicapped teenagers and young adults. Implemented this program which included areas.

Developed and implemented a program for handicapped teenagers and young
adults which included provisions for the blind, mentally retarded, and
cerebral palsied.

SUMMARY: Allowed me to understand the responsibility in my profession
for the first time. Introduced me to the skills of analysis of needs
of the development of programs to meet them. Also my first administrative training occurred at this time.

ABSTRACT OF EXPERIENCE

Experience, education, and training have developed my skills in these
areas of counseling:

Administration

Decision and Policy Making
Budget Analysis and Spending
Personnel Coordination
Responsibility

Program Development

Research
Design
Implementation
Evaluation

EDUCATION

B.S.   Wayne State University, Detroit (1961)

Major: Psychology
Minor: Business Administration
G.P.A. 3.3

M.S.   California State University, San Francisco (1966)

Major: Counseling
Minor: Social Work
G.P.A. 3.6

Thesis Title: "The Role of the Rehabilitation Counselor
Continuing Employment Placement: A Follow-Up Study of
Three Cases"

(Ph.D.)   University of Southern California, Los Angeles

Major: Counseling
Minor: Urban Studies
G.P.A. 3.8

Progress: All course work and examinations completed;
ABD—All but dissertation.

Projected Completion Date: June 1977

Dissertation Title: "An Experimental Program for the
Increased Affectiveness of the Rehabilitation Counselor
in Industry"

ADDITIONAL EDUCATION

Also studied advanced T-group and sensitivity training at the Western
Behavioral Sciences Institute (1966), the Langley Porter Neuropsychiatric
Institute (1967), and the Esalen Institute (1970).

PUBLICATIONS

"Teenagers and Parental Bias," Counseling Digest, V, 2 (June 1968),
   8-12ff.

"Rehabilitating Counselors," Impact Magazine, VII, 4 (August 1970),
   12-26.

"Where Do You Go Now?" Professional Guidance Journal (Winter, 1971),
    7-14

PERSONAL INFORMATION

    Marital Status: Married   Social Security Number: 770-34-991

    Birthdate: July 19, 1939   Dependents: None

EXERCISES

1. Discussion topics:

    a. What is the purpose of a resume?

    b. Does everyone need one? Why? Why not?

    c. How personal should a resume be?

    d. How often should it be updated?

    e. Why is the layout of a resume important?

    f. Why is information placed in blocks?

    g. How long should a resume be? Why?

    h. What is the distinction between "optional" and "required" information?

    i. What is the advantage of a prose resume?

2. You are a graduating senior. Using facts from your own background and experience, prepare a personal resume for mailing. Use the principles of selection, placement, and overall appearance discussed in this chapter.

3. When you are satisfied with your resume, make a second copy but delete your name. Exchange resumes with another student in your class and evaluate the resume you receive. What impression does it give of the writer? Which items are strongest? weakest? Which points are most positive? most negative? Be prepared to justify your criticism in class discussion.

4. Study the classified ads in several newspapers for openings in your field of interest. Make a list of the most frequently stated requirements for these positions. How well does your own experience coincide with your findings? Modify your basic resume to reflect your analysis.

5. Non-job-related experience can be relevant to required skills in employment. Meet with another student and take turns questioning each other about activities and interests outside your specific areas of education and employment experience. You may want to begin with a discussion of the items listed in the section headed "The Related Skills and Activities Block." Make a list of the activities and interests that apply to your career directly or indirectly.

6. List five qualities, applicable to other jobs, that you could acquire from each of the following positions: boxboy, taxi driver, gardener, factory worker, nurse's aide, sales clerk, typist, file clerk, cashier, bartender, service-station attendant, musician. Do the same for positions you have actually held.

7. Make a list of "required" and "desired" qualifications for the job description in Figure 1.4, Chapter 1. How does this list compare with the list made from Figure 2.3 in this chapter?

8. Call on a duplicating firm in your area and get an estimate on duplicating a specific number of resumes. Compare the various methods available for reproduction of resumes—photocopying, offset printing, mimeograph—and decide which would be best for you. Explain your choice.

The Application Letter 3

A Communication Bridge

What is the function of an application letter?
What should it say?
What should it look like?
Should I mention salary?
Should I use the pronoun "I"?
How can I improve my letter-writing style?
Should I use a form letter?

The application letter represents the next step in establishing communication between employer and applicant. In many employment situations a resume alone is sufficient, but in others, particularly those involving salary negotiations, a cover letter should be sent with the resume to form a complete application package. The purpose of this letter is to supplement the resume by summarizing the potential value of the applicant. The resume itemizes relevant information about the applicant. The letter of application should focus this data with respect to a specific job, and contain a request for an interview.

GOALS OF THE LETTER

The ultimate goal of the application letter is to obtain for the applicant a personal interview with the employer—the interview usually being the last step before a hiring offer is made. Therefore, your letter should stimulate the reader into wanting to talk personally with you. To develop a strong and positive application package, design your letter to accomplish the following aims:

1. <u>Attract attention</u>. Arouse the reader's interest. Try to associate your name with a specific job in the reader's mind.

2. <u>Reaffirm your qualifications</u>. Briefly summarize your background and experience in terms of the particular position. True, the information in the resume was included because it was relevant to the particular position (assuming the applicant followed the procedures in Chapter 2). But an outright explanation of that relevance is appropriate in the letter. Draw conclusions from the

items in the resume and assure the reader that you can handle the job. Point out specific examples of your past performance and ability. Offer references to vouch for your qualifications.

    3. <u>Anticipate and alleviate hesitation</u>. You may choose to answer any questions here that might cause the reader to think twice about seeing you, such as why you left your previous employer. (NOTE: If these questions are not mentioned here, they will certainly come up during the interview. Be ready for them!)

    4. <u>Arouse action</u>. Keep communication open by requesting a personal interview. Ask if you might visit or phone. Employ whatever device you feel is appropriate, within the parameters of good taste, to elicit a positive action from the reader.

    Employers want to hire qualified professionals who are sure of themselves and their abilities. Do not use the letter as a brag sheet, but avoid depreciating your own abilities or whining about your present employment (or unemployment) situation. Timorous appeals to an employer's sympathy are rarely effective. Never feel that you have to apologize for applying for work. Notice the balanced tone in the letter in Figure 3.1.

    We hear a great deal today about motivation. In the context of the application letter, you are presumably motivated to write by your understanding of the employer's needs. Your letter should reflect that understanding; therefore, you should take care to identify the employer's needs accurately. Generally the most successful application letters establish a common bond between the applicant and the employer. They focus resume information, reinforce points of strength, and freely explain any negative items that might naturally occur to the reader, such as a lack of experience or specific training. As with the resume, decide which items should be covered in the application letter by referring to the job description. Ask yourself these questions:

    What are the goals of this employer?
    How do these goals relate to me?
    What do I have in common with the employer?

Supplement your answers with information drawn from your personal observations of human nature, your knowledge of what employers are generally concerned with, and your research into the particular organization. From this information you can begin to plan the best strategy for your application letter. Decide on a tone, for instance, that reflects the qualities the reader is searching for to fill the position. Should the letter sound aggressive? dignified? casual? Answers to such questions will give you a real starting point when it comes to shaping and composing the letter.

CONTENT ANALYSIS

    Business letters usually have three functional parts: (1) the *introduction*, (2) the *body*, and (3) the *conclusion*. (These message elements do not necessarily correspond with separate paragraphs.) They roughly follow this general sequence:

FIGURE 3.1. A sample letter of application.

881 Walnut Park Drive
Rowley, MA 01969
January 21, 1976

Ms. Carroll Haynes
Personnel Officer
Matlock Publishing Company
Suite 104, Tower Building
Chicago, IL 60610

Dear Ms. Haynes:

Can I interest you in a young, intelligent woman who wants to carve out a
career with a progressive company? I have earned a college degree and have
already worked as a university teacher, researcher, a secretary, a legal
assistant, and an administrative assistant. At age 26 I am capable of learning well and can grow with an organization such as yours.

As a "management trainee," I could contribute while learning. I have
already helped set up a real estate department for a large mortgage company.
My administrative background so far includes preparation of legal documents,
delegation of work assignments and arrangement of work schedules, recruiting
and training, and research and clinical studies. I have served well as the
liaison between clients and office personnel.

I am an articulate person, I believe, and a good correspondent and motivator
of people. I will relocate and can travel as required.

Have I interested you? A phone call or letter will enable us to meet to see
how I do fit. Please contact me.

Sincerely,

A. T. Lee

(Ms.) A. T. Lee

ATL/JW

```
Let me introduce myself . . .
I am applying for the position of . . .
My reasons for applying are . . .
Can we discuss it further . . .
```

As you can see from this skeletal list of elements, the successful application letter clearly supplements the resume and leads directly to a personal interview.

THE INTRODUCTION

The opening paragraph in any letter has particular significance. It establishes the reader's impression *and* expectations for what is to follow. In an application, the purpose of the initial section is to introduce the applicant and identify the position being sought. It acts as a preface in both content and tone. A successful opening paragraph engages the reader's interest and then merges smoothly into the body of the letter.

Sometimes students find that the first sentence in a letter of application is the most difficult to write. Remember that in the most effective letters the writer immediately identifies the purpose of the message and establishes a common bond between the writer and the reader. Often, simply mentioning the source of the lead is sufficient. What led you to write the letter? Was it the strength of the company's reputation? The advice of a colleague or professor? Was it an advertisement in a newspaper or journal? Whatever the connection between the applicant and the prospective employer, identify and use it in the introductory phase of the letter.

In the detailed discussion that follows, three types of letter openings are analyzed: the direct, the modified direct, and the indirect. For convenience, they are arranged *from the least to the most desirable*. Note that this section contains both weak and strong samples. Refer to these openings when preparing your own letter and select whichever one fits your needs.

The Direct Opening

The *direct opening* is a simple, straightforward statement:

```
My name is _____ and I'm applying for . . .
Please accept my application for . . .
This is my application for . . .
May I please be considered for . . . ?
I feel qualified for . . .
My background and experience prepare me for . . .
Do you have an opening for . . . ?
My goal is to become a . . .
I am applying for . . .
```

The direct opening quickly identifies the position being sought, but it may be overly blunt in situations where tact or writing ability are desirable. Also, this approach tends to be dominated by the personal pronoun (see discussion later in this chapter), and characterized by a certain awkwardness and lack of originality. Avoid using this introduction if you can.

The Modified Direct Opening

The *modified direct opening* softens the abruptness of the direct opening by employing an introductory phrase prior to the identification of the position desired. This approach demonstrates more sophisticated writing style, since its overall tone is less harsh. The modified direct opening is almost always preferable to the direct opening:

With twelve years employment experience in the accounting field, I feel qualified to apply for . . .

After reading your advertisement in the New York Times, I am applying for the position of . . .

Because of my extensive background in the areas described in your employment description, may I be considered for . . . ?

Would you take a few moments to read through my qualification for the position of . . . ?

With June rapidly approaching, and with it the completion of my degree in data processing, I wish to apply for . . .

Mr. Blackstone, a former associate of your company, suggested that I contact you for . . .

Should there be an opening currently in your accounting department, please accept this application . . .

The Indirect Opening

The *indirect opening* is the most subtle of all, for it begins with an entire sentence—either complimenting the company or analyzing the position available—prior to a direct or modified direct statement of application. This approach shows the most thoughtfulness and demonstrates the most skill. It allows the applicant to bring pertinent information, directed toward the needs of the employer, into the letter immediately. A difficulty with the indirect opening, though, is that it can easily be overwritten. Avoid making it too cute, too polite, or simply too wordy.

In engineering design circles, Radius Associates has acquired an enviable reputation for creative approaches in electronic design. As an experienced engineer, I would be pleased to be considered for . . .

In a recent advertisement your organization emphasized a desire to hire young, aggressive college graduates for management training. I wish to be considered for . . .

Experience has taught me that a continuous record of good annual financial reports is an excellent indicator of a company's future. Do you presently have an opening for a CPA, who will work to continue this fine record?

THE BODY OF THE LETTER

In the body of the application letter you are expected to speak on your own behalf, citing reasons why you should be considered for the position. Here you should make direct statements stressing your individual qualifications (see Figure 3.2). Analyze your background in relation to the job at hand and discuss your individual goals, attitudes, and personal qualities. You may mention your willingness to relocate or your desire for advancement here to show that you have given the job sincere thought. You might also discuss your last employment and your reasons for leaving, though at this point such information is optional. As a general rule, avoid emotional appeals or references to other applicants.

The information presented here should either summarize or draw conclusions from data presented in the resume. Modified sales psychology is appropriate in this letter: Be positive and reinforce your best points. Identify your strongest assets and present them clearly. If you have a number of qualifications, however, do not discuss them individually in detail; repeating the objective data itemized in the resume will dilute the total effect of your letter. Choose one or two of your more convincing points and expand on them; rely on the resume or the personal interview for emphasizing the rest. (See Figure 3.8, later in this chapter, for an example of how to refer the reader to the resume.)

THE CONCLUSION

The final paragraph similar to the first, has an added impact on the reader due to its position in the letter; che closing statement leaves the last impression. Use this opportunity to urge the reader to continue the correspondence. If the preceding sections of the letter have been successful, it will be apparent to the reader that you should be contacted for an interview. In other words, if you have presented a positive impression of yourself in terms of the specific job at hand, the reader will not be inclined to hesitate on the grounds that certain information is not present, your letter is vague, or you "do not seem to be a person we're looking for." Use your last statement to imply that communication between you and the employer should remain open, and that the next move is up to the employer.

Politely request that the reader take a *specific* action: either setting up an appointment for a personal interview or—delaying the process by one step—providing further information.

FIGURE 3.2. A sample letter emphasizing statements of personal
qualifications in the body of the letter.

5121 Ranchito Avenue
Oklahoma City, OK 73052
December 11, 1975

Oklahoma Dome Oil Company
The Oklahoma Building
567 W. Manhattan Place
Oklahoma City, OK 73060

Gentlemen:

Your ad for "innovative systems analysts" in your new Synthetic Crude and
Minerals Division is the most exciting career opportunity ad I have read!
Let me explain why:

First, I like your company. I have worked for you before (from January 1967
to August 1968), and feel an affinity for the company and its goals.

Second, I like your problem. I not only identify with the computer aspects
of it, but I also appreciate the needs of the eventual users of the information system. I have a B.S. degree and an M.S. degree from the University
of Wisconsin. My majors were geology and data processing.

Third, I like your technology. After leaving your employ, I spent several
years in the design and implementation of large scale data base systems. I
then spent a year at my own expense designing minicomputer systems.

Fourth, I like your request for "innovative systems analysts." Several of
my supervisors have described my services in that way.

I look forward to an interview at your earliest convenience, to discuss
prospective employment with you.

Sincerely yours,

L. L. Waterman

L. L. Waterman

Notice that the examples of concluding sentences below fall into two categories. The first type is passive; in this conclusion you ask the employer to take the action and to contact you. The second category is more aggressive; here you assume he will want to meet with you. In this latter case, demonstrated in the last two examples below, the reader must take action not to meet with you.

May I hear from you in the near future regarding the possibility of an interview? My home telephone number is (555) 777-8383. I am normally home after 6:00 in the evening. Please call.

If you are interested in my qualifications for this position, I will be available at any time next week to meet with you in person.

If you will send me the information concerning the days that your representative will be in this part of the country, I will make arrangements for an interview.

I will make an appointment with you next week, at your convenience, if I do not hear from you to the contrary, to discuss my qualifications in more detail.

I am planning to be in your area a week from this Thursday, and will make an appointment with your secretary early in the week for a personal interview.

THE ELEMENTS OF A BUSINESS LETTER

What follows is a detailed description of the parts of a standard business letter. Each element has come into conventional usage based upon its function and the convenience of using a standard form. See Figure 3.3 for a summary of this information.

RETURN ADDRESS

When you do not use letterhead paper (that is, paper with a preprinted address and logo), the return address most often appears above the date or immediately below the signature block.

Include the zip code. This information may be found in the *National Zip Code Directory* (POD Publication 65).

States should always be identified with the standard two-letter abbreviation. (See Appendix C.)

DATE

Dates are reference points for both the applicant and the prospective employer. Most companies file and process applications by the date of receipt on a first-come first-serve basis.

You should keep a mailing log, showing when applications were sent. You can then record responses to gauge interest and prepare follow-up letters or calls if necessary. (See Chapter 5, Figure 5.4.)

FIGURE 3.3. Sample letter layout.

```
                                                   Address of Sender
                                                    Date of Letter
                                        (These elements may also appear
                                        flush left, above the inside address.
                                        The address of sender may alterna-
                                        tively appear beneath the sender's
    Inside Address                      name.)



    Salutation:

    Text of the Letter



    1.  Introduction



    2.  Body of the Letter



    3.  Conclusion





                                        Complimentary Close

                                            (Signature)

                                        Name of Sender
                                        Address of Sender (alternate)




    Initials (when typed by someone other than the applicant)

    Notation of Enclosures
```

Inside Address

This is an exact duplicate of the complete address of the recipient as it appears on the mailing envelope. It should include the name *and* title, if available, of the person in charge of hiring or interviewing.

Directing your letter to a specific addressee saves considerable time, since a correctly addressed application need not be shuffled from desk to desk. Names and titles of company officers, if not included as part of the job description, can be found with a little research (see Chapter 1).

Salutation

Once again, a specific name is most appropriate, although nominals—"sir," "gentlemen," "Ms.," "Mrs."—may be used when you have not been able to track down a specific name. To avoid sex-biased salutations in such cases, you may also use "Dear Advertiser," or "Dear Personnel Director." The salutation should be followed by a colon.

Body

The message of the letter should be single spaced, with a double space between paragraphs. Paragraphs may be indented or not, depending on your preference. The current convention is not to indent.

Some businesses adopt the style of a full left-hand margin in which all parts of the letter, including the return address, date, and signature, are flush with the left margin. Again, this choice is up to you.

Complimentary Close

The complimentary close represents a brief and simple courtesy. Avoid lengthy, old-fashioned compliments, such as "many thanks for your kind interest" or "I remain truly yours." "Sincerely" or "Yours truly" is appropriate and sufficient.

Signature Block

Sign the letter in ink, preferably black. Immediately below your signature, type your name to avoid confusion or error in reading your handwriting.

Initials

It is a business convention for the typist to place the writer's initials in caps plus his or her own initials in lower-case letters—PV:msl—at the bottom of the page for reference. This practice is optional in the application letter.

Enclosures

If the letter is accompanied by additional material, the reader is sometimes alerted by a notation in the lower left-hand corner of the page just below the initials; usually, "1 enclosure," or simply "Enclosure" is sufficient. Although resumes are usually enclosed with letters of application, this device is usually not used in application letters.

VISUAL ASPECTS

Each of us at one time or another has dressed up to meet a stranger. On such occasions we take special care with our physical appearance. This situation is analogous to writing an application letter. Since an application precedes a personal interview and therefore conveys a first impression to an employer, it should be neat, clean, and mechanically flawless. Neither grammatical errors nor typographical oversights should be allowed to mar or detract from the quality of your letter. If such errors do slip by your attention, the letter could act as a liability instead of an asset.

Studies suggest that the ability to spell may not necessarily reflect intelligence or professional capability. Nevertheless, a reader may consider misspelled and mistyped words in a letter as indications of the writer's lack of care and attention to detail. Letters of application and resumes are generally brief; usually the two together amount to no more than a few pages. Therefore, no matter how poorly you usually spell, there is no reason to allow errors to appear in your application package. Check the spelling and definition of every word you are not sure of in a current college-level dictionary.

If spelling is a particular problem for you, supplement your personal library with a specialized dictionary, such as Webster's *New World Word Book*, a compact listing of 30,000 words and common spelling variations, or *50,000 Words*, compiled by Henry Sharp. These books are designed specifically to be convenient spelling references. They contain no definitions or other extraneous information, and easily fit into a purse, a briefcase, or the corner of a desk drawer.

Keep in mind that a typographical error, such as *hte* or *tthe*, is as much of an error in the eyes of a reader as a misspelled word. Never mail your letters or resumes without proofreading them very carefully, word for word. Even then a gremlin or two may slip by you, so to be truly certain, find someone to help you with the final proofreading. Ask a friend to read your work critically and catch all errors while they are simple to correct.

Grammar is a broad subject, beyond the scope of this book. If you have any questions concerning correct English usage, consult any accepted reference book on the subject (see the Bibliography). If you plan to do a lot of writing, by all means purchase a grammar guide or check one out at your local library. Ask the librarian to help you select one.

It is impossible to overemphasize the importance of technical perfection and a neat appearance in application packages. For example, when many applications are received for the same position, a personnel director often begins the initial screening by eliminating all letters and resumes that look sloppy or contain misspellings and errors in grammar. Why risk a job for carelessness alone?

LETTER-WRITING STYLE

In the preceding sections the separate elements in an application letter were discussed in detail. In this section another, more subtle level of communication is treated: the overall psychological impact of the letter.

FIGURE 3.4. Another sample letter of application, demonstrating the elements in a standard business letter.

P.O. Box 814
East Lansing Station
East Lansing, MI   48823
USA
June 24, 1976

A. M. Webber, President
Thompson Manufacturing
R.R. #87
Claremont, Ontario, Canada

Dear Sir:

I believe my education and experience in the field of Operations Management could make me significantly valuable to your company as a member of your staff. I have proven capabilities and experience in the areas of finance, information systems, operations analysis, and capital-resource management.

I have a Bachelor of Science degree in Business Administration with a specialization in quantitative methods. I also have a Master of Science degree in Business Administration with a specialization in quantitative methods and information systems. Following these degree programs I took postgraduate courses in simulation techniques and finance.

Since I received my M.S. degree, I have had five years of business experience as both a consultant to clients and a staff member. My assignments have included work in the areas of production-management information systems and measurement of alternative investment strategies.

At present I am a vice president of a small consulting firm responsible for client consulting and product development and maintenance. While these responsibilities have been rewarding in many ways, I find that this position does not afford me the opportunity to fully utilize my capabilities nor my potential for long-term personal growth. For this reason, I am exploring other alternatives.

I have enclosed a brochure which provides more detailed information about my background and capabilities.

May I meet with you or a member of your staff to explore further my potential service to your company?

I look forward to hearing from you.

Sincerely,

Thomas G. Orr

TGO:yl

Read the letter of application in Figure 3.5. What sort of impression do you have of the writer? Even if you disregard the obvious lack of writing skill, you will probably be left with certain reservations as to Mr. Avery's professional qualifications. Consider the effect this employee would have on others. Would he reflect well on the company? The secretary who opens such a letter probably does not even pause to ask these questions before "filing" the application in the wastebasket.

Mr. Avery's letter lacks substance as well as character. It tells nothing at all about the writer, and does not even refer the reader to a resume for information. Overall, the letter makes the kind of impression that every writer should strive to avoid: Mr. Avery seems sloppy, careless, abrupt, and unconcerned about the reader's reaction to his letter.

In the improved version of this letter, Figure 3.6, the essential information has been included; consequently, the letter has a great deal more substance. It has a more professional character and gives the reader a much more complete picture of the applicant. The letter is correct from the standpoints of goals, content, physical make-up, and mechanics, but it still falls short of excellence. The style of the letter could be vastly improved. With a little time and effort and careful attention to the following elements of style, Mr. Avery could produce a very impressive application letter:

1. Tone
2. Individuality
3. Word usage
4. Paragraph flow
5. Emphasis

A third and final draft of Mr. Avery's letter (Figure 3.9) appears immediately following the discussion of these points. Compare this final version with the second letter and note that its style and depth make it obviously superior.

TONE

An application should be written in a formal, courteous, and tactful tone. Courtesy is simply the respect one person pays another in human relations; in business it is considered to be the hallmark of the professional. The conventions of professional courtesy do not imply that as an applicant you occupy an inferior position, or that you should adopt a fawning, introverted, or timid posture. Instead, they simply require you to employ the same gestures of courtesy that you would appreciate from others.

Tact is a slightly different application of the same principle: It is the thoughtful avoidance of subjects that could be embarrassing to the reader or, in some instances, to the writer himself. Being tactful does not mean you should *never* discuss certain issues. Rather, it is a matter of timing: The tactful person waits for the appropriate time to mention sensitive subjects, and then brings them up as thoughtfully as possible. Thus, it would be tactless to point out to an interviewer errors of judgment that you have observed within the company. But if you were invited to explain how you would handle a problem, you could tactfully contradict company policy in proposing your solution. Tact is the acquired ability to recognize the best time and manner of bringing up potentially emotion-laden subjects.

Determining the most tactful approach depends to some extent on the individual situation. In Figure 3.7, for example, the positive, even aggressive, tone has been exaggerated purposely. This

FIGURE 3.5.   A very poor letter of application.

13   Feb   1976

Alex Calbe Co.

Dear Sir

     In answer to your ad in the LATimes and communication with your personal dptm Iam applying for the position of mechnianical engineer.   I hope that you will give my application kind consideration.

Yours

James Avery

James Avery

FIGURE 3.6. An improved draft of the letter in Figure 3.5.

48 Edward Drive
Pomona, CA 91768
January 14, 1975

Mr. Albert C. Islas
Division Superintendent
State of California
Air Resources Board
9528 Telstar Avenue
El Monte, CA 91731

Dear Mr. Islas:

I am applying for the position of assistant evaluations engineer with the El Monte Division of the Air Resources Board. I will be graduating from California State Polytechnic University, Pomona, in June and getting married. Therefore, a job with the ARB would be very desirable for me at this time.

I am completing a major in mechanical engineering with an emphasis on automotive mechanics. I have taken courses in Heat Power, Combustion Engines, and Machine Design. I have some background in laboratory work and testing, including a course in Advanced Engineering Measurements.

Presently, I am completing my senior project, which consists of a carburetion problem.

My work experience of the last two summers has not been related to automotive engineering, but it was at Brockway Glass Company. In the summer of 1972, I worked as a packer. Last summer I was in charge of the maintenance of a variety of plant machinery and was able to suggest some design modifications to reduce machine breakdowns.

If you find that my qualifications are adequate, I hope I may hear from you.

Sincerely,

James Avery

James Avery

FIGURE 3.7. A sample letter with an aggressive tone.

4721 Brooks Drive
Cedar City, UT 84720
September 19, 1976

Mr. Richard Harvey
Personnel Director
SPACECO Computers
Cedar City, UT 84720

Dear Mr. Harvey:

My name is Joe Testerman, and I'm a Senior in the Humboldt State University
School of Business. My major is Marketing with a specialization in mass
media advertising and sales promotion. I plan to complete my bachelor's
degree by June of next year.

While studying modern management techniques in my world marketing class this
quarter, I became acquainted with your firm. I was very impressed by the
decisive manner in which SPACECO expanded its time-sharing marketing operations in the West—buying out the facilities of the sagging Semaphore Corporation, with its excellent plant and technical staff, and installing your own
management team to implement new policies. Congratulations! Last quarter's
earning reports as reported in Barron's shows a fine 8.2 percent gain in
gross profits.

I would enjoy working for a firm like SPACECO—a young company that is
prepared to expand decisively along opportunity growth lines. I would like
to join your team and grow with you.

Would it be convenient for me to meet with you in your office next week?
I'll call your secretary on Monday for an appointment.

Sincerely,

Joe Testerman
Joe Testerman

style would probably be inappropriate and considered tactless in most situations. But it does show an orientation toward the future and self-assurance that are far from negative qualities. This letter would not be effective for a staid, conservative corporation, but is it really too strong for someone interested in sales promotion? What does it tell you about the person who wrote it? Do the qualities of youth and enthusiasm outweigh the brashness in the tone? Would training and age help? In most cases, you should try to achieve a positive tone without relying on aggressiveness, patronization, appeals to sympathy, humor, or clever phrases. But remember that some situations can tolerate a heavier dose of such qualities than others.

INDIVIDUALITY

In Chapter 1 it was noted that many job seekers indiscriminately send out an identical form letter of application to every lead and hope for the best. This approach is the most common because it is the easiest, but it is certainly not designed for maximum effect. Refer to the example of such a form letter in Figure 3.8. Note that its tone is stiff and mechanical. Does the letter tell you anything about the writer? What? Hundreds of these applications, usually photocopied or mimeographed, pass across a personnel officer's desk every year, but few of them are ever answered. Form letters must contain only the most general information; they cannot be specific simply because of their wide distribution. They are vague and impersonal because they have not been designed to fit the situation. Consider now what additional information could be included to arouse further interest in the applicant as an individual, not as a stereotyped job candidate.

Your objective should be to make your letter stand out from others without being flashy. Above all, you should attempt to include information that is relevant to the position at hand and that introduces you as an individual, and not as a set of statistics on a resume. For example, you may decide to expand upon your experience, and include details that do not appear in the resume, to show the reader that you are truly a professional in your field. Consider the following response to an advertisement for a management position that requires computer background; the applicant shows that he had quite sophisticated experience in computer evaluation and trouble-shooting:

I was also responsible for evaluating manual operation systems for the purpose of recommending possible computerization of patient accountability. I then served as head of a search and standards committee in the selection of computer firms that would meet our requirements, supervised the installation of the new equipment, and then prepared the evaluation report after the first quarter of operation.

Think about the aspects of your personality or past experience that make you unique. Then present these unique qualities as assets.

Another excellent way to tailor your application letter to the specific situation is to use the knowledge you have about the company (see research section, Chapter 1) to show the reader that you clearly choose to work for them.

FIGURE 3.8.   A sample form letter.

---

86 Brier Road
Brooklyn, NY 11217
(212) 987-5567

Dear

    I will be graduating from the New York University Master's Degree Program in June of this year and I am actively seeking a position in any area of drama or related theater technology or a position instructing in these areas. I'm enclosing a resume, complete as of February, 1976, and I ask to be considered for jobs you may have open at this time, or any openings that may become available in the future.
    I'd like to arrange an appointment at your earliest convenience, at which time I could show you some samples of my work and look at your facilities.

Thank you,

John Hays.

John Hays

Word Usage

It is important that you adapt your language and writing style to the situation. An application letter should be composed with easy comprehensibility as the primary objective. There should be a suggestion of formality in the tone, as in the tone you might adopt in speech on a serious occasion. Avoid the urge to impress the reader with your vocabulary, but do not, on the other hand, fill your letter with slang, clichés, and contractions. Both of these extremes lead to an artificial tone which usually misrepresents the applicant. Use familiar words in common use to insure that your letter will be precise and easy to read. Also, avoid technical language or professional jargon whenever possible, for they make a letter sound dull and ponderous.

When you are responding to a detailed job description, employ the terminology used there to describe your qualifications. Not only will you characterize yourself as a desirable candidate, with this approach, but you will also insure against the possibility of being misunderstood. Besides, choosing the right words will be easier if you use the job description as a guide.

Words have two levels of meaning: the dictionary definition, and the emotional connotations. For example, the words "quit" or "fired" may be accurate for explaining why you left your last job, but they do carry a harsh emotional meaning. Other words—such as "terminated" or "gave notice" say the same thing in a less abrupt way; at times an entire phrase is necessary to soften the message. Explanatory phrases such as "Due to economic restraints . . . " or "necessary cutbacks arising from loss of contracts . . . " not only convey the original message to the reader, but also provide the rationale for why you left your last position. Do not feel you have to avoid sensitive issues in your letters; simply use tactful language to desensitize them and convey the necessary information.

Avoid using vague language or clichés, such as "future rewards," "stimulating challenges" or "growth potential." Such phrases have lost their meaning due to over-use. They tell the reader very little—except that the writer tends to use the first words that come to mind. Notice how much more effective the following phrases are: "your company's successful expansion into the European market last year," "your recent managerial accomplishments in the XK proposal," or "the breakthrough in systems analysis that I read about in the November *Barron's*." These phrases admittedly take more thought and time to prepare, but the effect is worth the extra effort.

Paragraph Flow

A mention of paragraphing style, as related to letters, is appropriate here. The physical length of a paragraph can affect a reader's attitude. An extremely long initial paragraph, for example, may discourage the reader; it might give the impression of being too complicated and difficult to understand. Conversely, a one-sentence paragraph suddenly appearing in the middle of a letter will jar the reader, and its abbreviated structure could place an undue emphasis on the information it expresses.

A paragraph should be a fluid block of related information. The writer can control the length of paragraphs by adding or subtracting information. Information in an overly long paragraph need not be deleted entirely, but should be used to construct another paragraph. Letter writing has some conventions of its own which distinguish it from other forms of writing. Therefore, though good writing in general does not require short paragraphs, paragraphs in letters ought to be kept relatively brief; limit their length to two or three sentences. This rule of thumb should help you compose clear, readable correspondence.

Your application letter should flow smoothly, and not trudge from one point to another. Often a writer carefully builds each sentence and paragraph to fulfill certain requirements, but forgets to go back over the final product to see how well it all fits together. Thus, individual ideas may be well-expressed, but they stand alone instead of forming a unified presentation with the other ideas in the letter. You can guard against this common error by reading your letter aloud. In doing so any need for word bridges, called transitions, will become immediately apparent. Transitions are logical signposts that alert the reader to what is coming next. A simple way of testing your transitions to see how well they work is to move paragraphs about. If the paragraphs can be easily shifted from one part of the letter to another, then the transitions (as well as the structure as a whole) are probably weak. Notice in Figure 3.9 how each paragraph is joined smoothly to the next. Compare this letter to the version in Figure 3.6, where paragraphs stand virtually alone.

If you wish to read further about writing style, a fine little book in the subject is *Elements of Style* by William Strunk, Jr., and E. B. White.

STRUCTURING FOR EMPHASIS

The most effective business letters have a single, clearly developed purpose. You may use a letter to apply for a job opening, request further information, or reply to an employment offer. In each case the letter is designed around one central idea. The purpose of the letter, whether it is a question or a response, is referred to as the *thesis*. The following phrases express common theses:

In response to your request for information . . .
May I have a retirement and insurance brochure?
I am pleased to accept your offer . . .
Regretfully, I am unable to . . .
Please accept this application . . .

This statement of purpose may appear in different places within a letter. The placement of the thesis determines the emphasis it receives within the letter as a whole. When it comes early it is stressed heavily; if it comes later the supplementary information gains in importance.

If the thesis appears toward the beginning of the message, as it most often does in application letters, then the remainder of the message will be an expansion of the thesis through supplementary information. In this case, the structure is "deductive"; the writer introduces a general statement early and then shows it to be true as deduced from specific facts.

But if the thesis is delayed until the middle or even the conclusion of a letter, the supporting information appears first. This is called the "inductive structure"; it moves through a series of specific facts that lead to a final conclusion—the major purpose of the message, or its thesis. The pivotal point in the inductive approach is indicated by a semantic turning point,

FIGURE 3.9. An excellent version of the letter in Figure 3.6.

48 Edward Drive
Pomona, CA 91768
January 14, 1975

Mr. Albert C. Islas
Division Superintendent
State of California
Air Resources Board
9528 Telstar Avenue
El Monte, CA 91731

Dear Mr. Islas:

Because of my education in automotive engineering, interest in pollution control, and experiences in testing and evaluations, I feel I am qualified for the position of assistant evaluations engineer with your El Monte Division of the Air Resources Board. I will be immediately available for employment after graduating from California State Polytechnic University, Pomona, in June with a major in mechanical engineering emphasizing automotive mechanics.

My senior project—an independent design project encouraging research, testing, and evaluation—provided me with experiences relevant to the kinds of work you are doing in the testing and evaluation of antipollution devices. I designed an electrothermal heating element for a standard carburetor for increased engine efficiency. This was then tested and evaluated under the most advanced theories of engineering measurements, employing a computer program and statistical methods.

In addition to my formal education, I have had valuable work experience. Last summer, I was responsible for maintaining a variety of machines at Brockway Glass Company, and I suggested design modifications that significantly reduced machine breakdowns. This experience impressed me with the relevance of engineering skills, and with the need to convey suggestions clearly and persuasively to management.

After you have examined the enclosed resume, Mr. Islas, please call me at 374-4726 in the late afternoon or evening and name a time that I may come to El Monte to talk to you.

Sincerely,

James Avery

James Avery

which leads to an inevitable conclusion. The following words and phrases (conjunctions and transitional phrases) are common pivots of the inductive letter: accordingly, as a result, consequently, hence, however, in fact, therefore, and thus.

The advantage of the deductive technique is that it is straightforward; it follows a conversational line of development and is therefore easier to write. The inductive technique is more rhetorical and requires more planning; however, it allows an applicant to prepare the reader more thoroughly for the thesis. It delays the conclusion until a more complete framework of information has been presented. This structure is helpful when the writer wishes to soften the impact of a potentially abrupt message. Sensitive situations requiring this "softening-of-the-blow techniqe" are most often encountered after the placement interview, when an applicant is involved in subtle negotiations, follow-ups, or refusals of offers—problems which are discussed more fully in Chapter 5.

In the successful Avery letter, Figure 3.9, the writer employs a simple deductive structure. It begins with a direct statement, "I feel that I am qualified for the position." The next paragraphs demonstrate the premise from which the thesis was deduced. They focus attention on two expanded examples of the applicant's skill and preparation. The letter ends strongly by directing the reader to the resume for further support, and by requesting a personal interview.

CHECKING YOUR ROUGH DRAFT

While your letter of application is still in the draft stage prior to final typing and mailing, check through it to be certain that it has met the goals described. Does it fit in your overall application program? Is there any additional information that you want to present at this stage? Consider the letter as a bridge between the resume and the interview. As a transitional document, it should underscore your qualifications and smooth the way for an interview. Any items of information that you think could block an interview should be handled now and directly. If you were fired from a previous job, if you lack references, or if you have a felony record or a poor health record, explanations are in order. Explain these things directly and straighforwardly. But keep your explanations brief; do not allow them to become digressions that will distract from the overall purpose of the letter: the presentation of your qualifications.

Remember that an effective application letter should be prepared in terms of your individual analysis of the job you are seeking and the impression you wish to give to the reader. When you reread your application, examine it for these features:

1. Does it contain the factual material required?

2. Does it draw conclusions about your personal qualifications from the more detailed information on your resume?

3. Is it tailored to fit the particular job, and is it courteous?

4. Does it fit into your employment campaign—that is, does it aim for the kind of job you are seeking in the location you prefer?

5. Does it prepare the way for a personal interview?

6. Is it grammatically and technically perfect?

THREE COMMON PROBLEMS

Should I bring up salary? When and How?

May I use the pronoun "I" in the letter?

Is it permissible to polish the facts?

SALARY

It is advisable to avoid making specific salary demands during the early stages of the job-search process unless, as often happens, the job description or hiring advertisement requires applicants to state their salary expectations. This advice is based on a modified sales technique: Capture the prospective buyer's interest before mentioning cost. If you are required to state a figure, try to keep it inexact; state a range instead. It is very easy for a prospective employer, when initially screening your application, to disregard it on the basis of an "unrealistic" salary demand alone. Salary is your best bargaining point in negotiation. Don't agree to a figure until the employer commits himself to hiring you. When he or she shows an interest in you and your qualifications, you will have entered the bargaining state. This usually occurs at the time of the interview.

In some circumstances, however, you may not wish to be considered for employment below a certain salary. In such cases, you should state the desired salary or mention your past salaries in the resume or the letter of application. Indicate that you desire the position, but only above a certain amount. By so doing you invite the employer to accept or reject your terms from the beginning. In this situation it will be assumed that you already have a good idea of comparable salaries in your field. If you wish to state a minimum salary but are not really sure of the current pay scales in your field, review current job advertisements and employment bulletins to unearth this important information quickly.

THE PERSONAL PRONOUN

Applying for a job is one of those rare occasions when you will not be considered impolite if you talk about yourself. You are, in essence, the field representative for a product you know very well, and you are expected to sell it. Do not hesitate to use the word "I" whenever necessary in a letter of application or on a resume.

Stylistically, it is more graceful to refer to yourself in the first person rather than the third. Referring to yourself as "the applicant" can lead to some very awkward sentences. It can also lend an extremely formal, and sometimes even pompous, tone to the letter. It is possible to over-use any word, however, so try to avoid starting every sentence with "I."

The following examples might appear in either the resume or the letter. Try substituting third-person for first-person references and see how awkward these examples become.

I am interested in obtaining a position with a recognized public accounting firm. My goals are to expose myself to all aspects of work experience which would prove advantageous in preparing myself for a career as a Certified Public Accountant. It is also important that my position provide the necessary experience to fulfill the CPA requirements specified by the State Board of Accountancy.

I wish to enter a Management Trainee Program in a company such as yours, an organization whose personnel policies encourage advancement and promotion.

Telling the Truth

A job offer is usually based on the contribution the employer hopes you will make to the organization. The employer will use an assessment of your past as an index of your future productivity. Some people object to this type of prediction, but it is a convention that is not likely to disappear in the near future. Decisions affecting your career will be made upon, and largely affected by, the information you supply in your resume or letter of application. Since you are responsible for preparing these documents, you have sole discretion over what is included—that is one of the governing principles of this book. But if you include information that is in any way untrue or misleading, you overstep the boundaries of discretion and enter the area of unethical manipulation.

Absolute sincerity, with yourself and others, is a basic requirement in the job-search process. You might be strongly tempted from time to time, to make a clean start by glossing over difficulties, improving on the facts, or simply failing to mention deficiencies in your past. We all wish we could alter our backgrounds, at least a little. But lying on a job application is reason enough for immediate dismissal, and self-deceit is equally dangerous. If you evaluate your own professional abilities dishonestly, you could easily convince yourself to go after the wrong job. Employers, reviewing your application with a more objective eye, would probably note the discrepancy and pass you over. All your job-search efforts might therefore be in vain unless you assess your abilities and interests honestly and try to find a job that matches that assessment.

Unsolicited Applications

If you are not content to wait for published job leads and wish to make the initial contact yourself, prepare a list of potential employers from newspapers, the telephone directory, or any of the other sources mentioned in Chapter 1, and start sending out material about yourself. The unsolicited application differs from the letter of inquiry, discussed in Chapter 1, in that it contains a resume and *provides* information instead of requesting it.

The unsolicited application is designed on the assumption that sooner or later all the employees of a particular company will be replaced. The sample letter that follows in Figure 3.10, therefore, begins with a question. Is this the time? Is there a job available to me now? It takes into account both possibilities—yes or no—through the use of conditional clauses:

FIGURE 3.10. An example of an unsolicited application.

P.O. Box 814
College Park, MD 20742
September 7, 1976

Mr. Jeffrey Numbers
Personnel Relations Manager
Elrex Pharmaceuticals
1763 W. Foothill Drive
Ames, IA 50010

Dear Mr. Numbers:

Would you be interested in hiring a sales manager who has college degrees in
both business management and pharmacy—and twenty years experience?

I have not quite achieved such eminent credentials yet, but these are the
qualifications I am striving to reach. Would you take the time to read my
resume and let me know if there is an opening now for me with Elrex?

[Normal Application Letter Development]

I would be able to travel to Ames in a few weeks for an interview, if you
have a position for me. However, if there is no opening now with Elrex,
would you please keep this application on file?

Sincerely yours,

Frances E. Nuss

Frances E. Nuss

> . . . if there is an opening now, please accept my application.
>
> . . . if there is no opening at this time, please keep my application on file for future reference.

A job seeker building a job-search campaign on unsolicited, or "blind," applications might send out anywhere from ten to a hundred "blind" letters. Since there is no way to estimate how many jobs are not advertised, it is difficult to evaluate the potential of this technique. But before you do decide to send out a substantial number of blind applications, weigh the investment against the return. All the letters will have to be individually typed and you will have to have an equal number of resumes duplicated; this could amount to a considerable expense, particularly when you consider that the return could be very small. Replies can be sparse—often as few as one out of ten. You would probably be more apt to beat the odds by placing your resume in an organization which you know has an opening.

ZIPPER LETTERS

The questionable value of form letters as compared with individually tailored applications was discussed earlier. Still, the form letter does have some points in its favor in certain circumstances—it saves time and is easy to prepare. The effect on the reader, however, is impaired by this very convenience; the form letter is just too impersonal. In this section we consider an alternative that combines the qualities of efficiency and effectiveness—the zipper letter.

The zipper letter is basically a form letter that has been designed to give the impression of individuality. In the form letter only the address and salutation is changed. But in the zipper letter, key segments are adjusted to fit the situation. Compare the form letter in Figure 3.11 with the zipper letter in Figure 3.12, noting that the underlined sections in the latter can easily be zipped in or out with each typing.

The advantage of the zipper-letter technique is that you need not write a new letter each time you apply for a job. You may reach an infinite number of potential employers using the same basic letter without impairing the quality of the message. The primary changes usually occur in the lead sentence, with a few substitutions scattered throughout the rest of the letter for consistency. But entire paragraphs can be zipped in and out in situations that require a great deal of individuality. This method requires a little more time for planning, and additional research will be required to make the interchanged segments effective. But the technique is well worth the effort; zipping can be used for applications, inquiries, follow-ups, requests for reference, or any other occasions in which the writer may decide to send out a number of similar letters.

A CHECKLIST FOR PREPARING AN APPLICATION LETTER

1. Is the letter brief and well-written?
2. Is it scrupulously neat? No strike-overs or erasures?
3. Is it addressed to a specific person? Is the name correct?

FIGURE 3.11. A sample form letter.

402 East D Street
Urbana, IL 61680
July 17, 1976

Dear

As a man who knows sales and promotion, you may be interested in taking a few
minutes to review the enclosed record of successful campaigns. I am sure it
will interest you.

My experience in equipment began with my first job as an operator. Since
then I have traveled to many foreign cities as sales representative for the
major manufacturers. Recently my work has been moving more heavily into
management where my knowledge has been applied to campaign promotions as an
administrative supervisor.

Would you kindly read my resume and allow me to arrange an appointment with
your secretary for next week?

Thank you for considering me for this position.

Yours truly,

Edward Thurman

FIGURE 3.12. A sample zipper letter.

402 East D Street
Urbana, IL 61680
July 17, 197

Mr. Maynard Carle
Vice-President,
Foreign Sales Division
Practor Equipment Sales
934-44 Benson Street
Bloomington, Illinois 61701

Dear Mr. Carle:

Product identification is a key to successful sales. As a professional, I
have watched with admiration Practor's use of the "gem logo" in national
magazine advertising.

As a man who knows sales and promotion, Mr. Carle, you may be interested in
taking a few minutes to review the enclosed record of successful campaigns.
I am sure it will interest you.

My experience in equipment began with my first job as a Practor operator.
Since then I have traveled to many foreign cities as sales representative
for the major manufacturers. Recently my work has been moving more heavily
into management where my knowledge has been applied to campaign promotions
as an administrative supervisor.

Would you kindly read my resume and allow me to arrange an appointment with
your secretary next week when I will be in the Bloomington area?

Thank you for considering me for a position with the Practor organization.

Yours truly,

Edward Thurman

Edward Thurman

4. Is the letter well-organized?

5. Does each sentence have a specific purpose?

6. Is the language appropriate? no clichés or slang?

7. Is the grammar correct? no misspelled words?

8. Is the overall tone appropriate?

9. Have all the important items been included?

10. Should anything else be included in the envelope?

EXERCISES

1. Discussion topics:

   a. What are the functions of an application letter?

   b. What information should be included?

   c. Why is the first line of a letter difficult to write?

   d. What is the best way to conclude an application letter?

   e. In what ways does an unsolicited letter differ from a normal letter of application?

   f. Is it possible to be *too* courteous?

   g. What motivates an application letter?

   h. Is it all right to use "I" in a letter?

   i. Should salary be discussed? When? How?

   j. What are the advantages of a form letter? disadvantages?

   k. How does word selection affect tone?

   l. How does paragraph length affect comprehension?

2. Prepare your own letter of application for a part-time or summer job.

3. Explain the advantages of a letter of application when used in conjunction with a resume. How would your resume have to be modified if it were not accompanied by a letter?

4. In accordance with what you have learned about structuring for emphasis, prepare two outlines for application letters containing these partial sentences:

   "I am applying for the position of . . . "
   "Therefore, I am applying for the position of . . . "

   How does the structure of each differ?

5. Write a letter of application *not* to be accompanied by a resume under the name Mr. Charles Marquis for a position as a retail shoe store manager. Do not identify yourself as the author. Read all the letters in the class aloud and vote on the three best. Discuss the characteristic of the letters that are chosen.

6. Write a critique on the two letters of application that follow (Sample A and Sample B). Rewrite these letters, making them more effective.

7. From the job descriptions cited earlier in Figure 1.2 and 1.3 (Chapter 1) make a checklist of items that should go in a letter of application.

Atlantic Services

Hello th ere ---

Idly looking thru some old papers and chanced to see you're nice ad requesting someone to work for your people. The notice reminds me of some work that
I did once for a similar group, and a good many things that have happened
since.

If you now have anyone than don't bother to get excited, because they are
probably good and/or have more experience. However, people have told me that
I am not lacking in efficiency, which is why I am trying to give almost perfect service to an employer, boss, etc.

I would imagine that you would also like to know that I have had many jobs
and experience. I have also had many good freinds who like what I do and
would be willing if you want to tell you too. The telephone company and the
mill. But the fact remains that you may wnat me to work for you and other
various needs.

As a practical matter, I would prefer to talk with you or someone about this,
thus saving you time and bookkeeping, and permitting me to bring some things
along should it be alright tomorrow. . .. or the next day about 11;00.

Let me know, or I'll call you about this.

                    Cordially,

                    Thomas Clark

                    Thomas Clark

Personnel Office
Superior Mills
Superior, OH 43212

Gentlemen:

In response to your ad of the 7th, I am taking a calculated risk by requesting an input meeting about the described position. Please review the resume appended, at your leisure, and see where I'm coming from.

I only want to say here that I work well with people and honestly feel qualified to meet your organization's needs. I would be honored to be associated with a dynamic and innovative company like Superior Mills. I am looking forward therefore to a fruitful and meaningful association in the future.

In conclusion, I will wrap up with these last words. I sincerely hope that you will be impressed positively by my background and frame of reference. I am anticipating my meeting with you, as soon as possible, at your convenience eagerly.

Sincerely yours,

Gail McMunn

Gail McMunn

The Personal Interview 4

A Face-to-Face
Meeting

What is an interview all about?
What qualities is the interviewer usually looking for?
How can I prepare myself beforehand?
What should I know about the company?
Should I bring anything with me?
What kind of questions should I expect?
What can I learn in the interview?

The personal interview, the face-to-face meeting between an applicant and a representative of
the hiring organization, is used almost universally by employers as the final stage in selecting
competent employees. The interview can be a nerve-racking experience for the applicant who does
not know what to expect, but the job seeker who understands the function of the interview can use
this meeting to advantage. For the applicant, the key to a successful interview is preparation.
Are you able to discuss yourself and your possible place in the company structure articulately and
self-confidently? What do you have to offer? Do you project the image of a responsible professional? What are your thoughts and attitudes? your goals for the future? your principles? None
of these items will appear on your resume, but all could contribute to your value as an employee.
The interviewer will be interested in information about the professional aspects of your personality—qualities that are less tangible than those you describe in the pages of typewritten information you prepared.

In this chapter the personal interview is analyzed from both the perspective of the applicant
and that of the employer. The kinds of information an interviewer is usually looking for, and the
steps you can take to prepare are identified and discussed in detail. Equally important, you are
encouraged to evaluate the experience and use this information later. The cardinal principle of
the interview approach described here is, learn to anticipate what will probably occur and be ready
for it. The interview is fundamentally a question-and-answer session about you, the job available,
and the company, so part of your preparation should involve determining information *you* might need,
and developing questions to ask the interviewer.

LEARNING ABOUT THE ORGANIZATION

Begin preparing for the interview by asking yourself what you know about the company or organization. Can you comfortably carry on an informed conversation with one of its representatives? If not, do a little homework. Applicants' lack of preparation in this area is the weakness most often cited by professional recruiters and personnel officers. From a pragmatic point of view, if an applicant does not know enough about the organization to discuss his or her future there the interviewer will probably wind up explaining the company's fundamental purpose. Interviewing time is too valuable to waste on such elementary explanations. And, poor impressions aside, the applicant should sincerely want to discuss the job and ask informed questions of the interviewer.

By the time of the interview the applicant should be informed about the company, and specifications of the job, such as requirements, salary, employee benefits, and working conditions. (See the sample list in Chapter 5.) This information can be found either in company literature or at the library. Refer to Chapter 1 for a discussion of how and where to acquire published data about various organizations. Some of the questions you may wish to answer for yourself are:

1. What is the company's major purpose—manufacturing, service, administrative?

2. What products does it produce, if any? for what markets?

3. Has the company made any significant gains or endured any reversals recently?

4. What is the organizational structure—linear, diversified, or conglomerate?

5. How does it fit into the broad economic structure?

6. Who are some of its major officers, board members, or stockholders?

7. How large is the organization? How many employees, subsidiaries, assets, or profits does it have?

8. What are their major interests in personnel hiring?

9. How old is the organization?

10. What is the company "image"?

You may not feel that all this data is necessary for gaining a sense of the organization. On the other hand, you may have some questions that you cannot answer yourself. If so, jot them down and ask the interviewer.

PERSONAL QUALITIES

Employment interviews are crucial in the continuing life of any company or organization; the success of all future operations hinges on the hiring decisions that grow out of them. Basically, the interviewers in a company—usually department managers or special personnel officers—are responsible for finding and screening the best possible candidates for open positions. They can then evaluate the applicants with respect to two sorts of information: qualifications and personal qualities. The former are found primarily in resumes and applications; the latter are discovered in personal interviews.

All interviewers operate on the assumption that people differ widely in terms of background, experience, attitude, and ability. Their job is to find and submit recommendations on applicants' distinctive characteristics. Interviewers are not always looking for specific answers, even when they ask direct questions; there is, after all, no model employee to be matched. Most often the interviewer is weighing intangible factors, such as personality traits, ideals, and attitudes, along with basic education and experience qualifications. The personal qualities required may differ greatly from position to position; for example, the qualities desired in a sales representative for a large chemical company would probably be quite different from those sought in a research engineer by the same firm.

Undesirable qualities with respect to employment generally fall into two categories: passive and aggressive. From the applicant's point of view, extremes in both categories should be avoided during the interview. In the descriptions that follow, the undesirable extremes of passive and aggressive behavior are analyzed so the reader can develop a perspective and see how individual traits combine to form a composite picture. The middle ground between these two extremes, called *positive neutral* behavior here, is composed of the most desirable traits. The reader should read carefully through each of these descriptions and, by evaluating his or her own personality traits in terms of the two extremes, try to reach a balance at the positive neutral point (see Figure 4.1.) NOTE: The categories of traits do not depict complete psychological profiles. Rather, they contain qualities that personnel interviewers generally consider important.

THE PASSIVE EXTREME—UNDESIRABLE

1. Displays a fawning, servile courtesy.

2. Speaks very little during the interview; answers only direct questions without elaborating.

3. Does not appear at ease; freezes up and acts very tense when addresssd directly.

4. Overemphasizes procedure and relies on others' instructions.

5. Is unable to express himself clearly; gives indefinite responses to questions; voices few opinions.

6. Displays little enthusiasm for anything; is indifferent; asks no questions about job or salary.

7. Has few outside interests or activities.

8. Is overly self-critical; makes excuses; apologizes, or is evasive about past job performance.

9. Fails to look interviewer in the eye; has a weak, limp handshake; avoids any physical contact.

10. Seems eager to end the interview.

11. Submits incomplete resume or application.

12. Seems pessimistic about the future. Generally displays negative attitudes and little sense of humor.

FIGURE 4.1. Balancing your personal qualities.

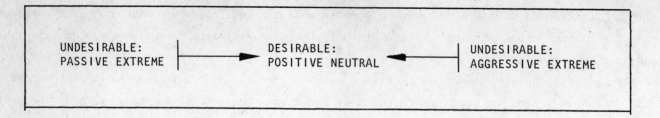

UNDESIRABLE: DESIRABLE: UNDESIRABLE:
PASSIVE EXTREME   POSITIVE NEUTRAL   AGGRESSIVE EXTREME

THE AGGRESSIVE EXTREME—UNDESIRABLE

1. Shows little courtesy or respect for the interviewer.

2. Dominates the conversation; talks a great deal, but does not seem to listen.

3. Uses high-pressure tactics to sell himself.

4. Exhibits forced humor; relies on stock stories and tries to be funny.

5. Displays little tact or appreciation for the feelings of others; speaks freely and critically about past associates and employers, and assumes intimacy.

6. Draws out the interview; makes elaborate promises.

7. Dislikes schoolwork and considers experience unimportant.

8. Tends to be impatient; does not accept criticism.

9. Knows very little about the company; seems only to be shopping for the best deal.

10. Intolerant of others; has narrow interests and strong prejudices.

11. Unwilling to start at the bottom; strongly egotistic.

12. Overemphasizes starting salary and fringe benefits.

13. Is unprepared for the interview; submits carelessly written resume; has not read company literature.

14. Dresses flamboyantly.

POSITIVE NEUTRAL BEHAVIOR—DESIRABLE

1. Arrives on time.

2. Remains courteous throughout the interview.

3. Values the interviewer's time. Ends the conversation with a recap of major points and thanks the interviewer for the time and attention.

4. Acts naturally and dresses neatly.

5. Articulates ideas well; displays poise and gives thoughtful responses to questions; looks the interviewer straight in the eyes.

6. Brings relevant documents to interview.

7. Shows qualities of maturity and confidence; has realistic plans for the future.

8. Has well-adjusted personal life.

9. Is interested in the company and the job; knows his or her field of specialization and is able to translate past experience into ideas relevant to the job at hand.

10. Asks relevant questions.

11. Listens to the interviewer carefully.

12. Is willing to discuss salary within the context of his or her own career *and* the requirements of the employer.

13. Generally has a positive attitude toward life.

INTERVIEW QUESTIONS

The questions an interviewer asks usually fall into two categories: the *closed* and the *open* inquiry. Your ability to recognize the distinction between these types will add greatly to the effectiveness of your responses. And noticing which type of inquiry the interviewer favors will give you some insight into the personality of the interviewer as well as the nature of the company he or she represents.

The *closed question* is a direct request for information:

"Have you ever been in the military?"
"What kind of work does your husband do?"
"When would you be able to start working for us?"

These questions normally occur toward the beginning of the interview. They are usually meant to help the applicant relax and enter into a natural conversation, while supplying the interviewer with relevant information. Answer closed questions directly and briefly; avoid building on them.

The *open question* is not meant to elicit specific information; it tends to shift the discussion into areas of attitudes and personal characteristics:

"Why did you choose to apply to us, rather than to IBM?"
"What do you see yourself doing in ten years?"
"What do you feel are the most important qualities needed by a department manager?"

These questions are more difficult to answer. The interviewer will ask them to draw you out, to see how much thinking you have done about your career in general and this job in particular. Take your time in answering them, and explain your responses carefully and thoroughly.

The following sections are composed of the most commonly asked questions in these two categories. When you look them over, pay particular attention to the open questions. Note that many of them have already been broached in the resume and letter of application. See if you would have any trouble responding fully without simply reiterating the written material. If you find some questions that you cannot answer easily, think about them for awhile; you might even jot down a few notes to take with you to the interview. But do not try to develop "pat" answers to these questions. You might be tempted to memorize responses; this would result in a forced and unnatural tone. Be sincere but tactful; and do not try to second-guess the interviewer by attempting to give responses you think he or she would like to hear. Above all, do not try to bluff your way through an answer if you do not have an answer. Be sincere enough to admit you don't know.

Following the two lists of sample interviewers' questions is a list of sample questions often asked by *applicants* in interviews. Scan the list and prepare some questions relevant to your own situation. Think of yourself as conducting a miniature interview within an interview. What do you want to know about the company before you agree to work there? Ask questions now.

SAMPLE CLOSED QUESTIONS

1. How do you spend your spare time?

2. Are you interested in sports? gardening? music?

3. Where were you raised?

4. Are you married? Do you have children? How old?

5. Is your husband or wife employed? Where?

6. What other jobs have you held?

7. Are you looking for a permanent position?

8. Do you like to work with others? by yourself?

9. What do you read? newspapers? magazines? books?

10. Were you ever in the military?

11. Did you enter activities at school?

12. What classes did you like best? least?

13. Where did you find this job lead?

14. Have you traveled extensively? Where?

15. Do you have references?

16. Would you be willing to relocate in another area?

17. Do you know anyone who works for us now?

18. Are your parents living?

19. What are your hobbies?

20. Are you involved in any civic activities?

SAMPLE OPEN QUESTIONS

1. How do you picture your career in five, ten, twenty years?

2. Why did you leave your last job?

3. What type of boss do you like?

4. Why did you apply to this particular company?

5. What do you know about us? about our competitors?

6. What have you learned from other jobs you have held?

7. Which do you feel is more important in your field, education or experience? Why?

8. What single factor do you think determines a person's progress in their professional career?

9. What personal qualities are necessary in your field? which are your strongest?

10. Do you consider yourself a creative person? analytical?

11. If you started college again, what would you take?

12. What type of people make you angry?

13. Do you have any difficulty being tolerant with other people who have different backgrounds or interests?

14. Would you be willing to start at the bottom?

15. What do you think your starting salary should be?

16. Did you have difficulty answering these questions?

17. What questions would you like to ask me?

SAMPLE APPLICANT QUESTIONS

1. How does one advance in this organization?

2. If I were required to relocate, how much of the expense would the company pay?

3. Is any overtime required for this position? How much? How is overtime compensated?

4. If I wished to go back to school at night, would the company pay any expenses? How much?

5. Could I withdraw my contributions from the retirement program if I left?

6. How permanent is this position?

7. Is there an incentive program for new ideas?

8. What is your policy on pregnancy leaves?

9. How independent would I be in this position?

10. Do I have a choice about where I would be assigned?

11. Will the company compensate me for use of my own vehicle? telephone? tools and supplies?

12. How does this company compare with its competitors?

13. Would my lack of education hold me back?

14. If I were laid off because of lack of work, would the company give me severance pay? help me find other work?

15. When will you be making a decision on this position?

16. Can I provide any further information?

SENSITIVE ISSUES

The question of sincerity was discussed in Chapter 3. It should be noted here that the personal interview is the time and place in which to clear up any ambiguity that might still exist with regard to your background or experience. The interviewer will want you to explain any breaks in the continuity of your work history and discuss sensitive items such as reasons for prior dismissal or personal problems that could affect your employability. Be prepared for direct open questions on these matters. Also, if you feel that the interviewer may overlook certain events in your past that need explanation, bring them up forthrightly.

A PERSONAL PLAN

A selection interview is a two-way process of communication. A professional interviewer is trained to be a good listener as well as an inquirer. It is his or her job to see that information is accurately transmitted in both directions. To aid in this process, consider preparing your own personalized interview plan. List your strongest qualifications for employment and the questions you wish to ask. Include your responses on abstract subjects, such as your personal fitness for the position, reasons for wanting to work for the company, and long-range professional goals. Then, during the course of your meeting with the interviewer, you can be ready to introduce this material whenever it is appropriate. Or, if the interviewer seems to be focusing on other things, you can see to it that these points are covered. If you find it difficult to keep everything in your mind, particularly in a face-to-face discussion, take your interview plan along. The use of notes is helpful and perfectly appropriate.

LEVELS OF COMMUNICATION

You should be prepared to respond to the interview situation as it develops. Normally, the interview evolves naturally from the expectations of the interviewer and the applicant. Both wish to exchange information; both also wish to make a strong impression, or, in the lexicon of industry and advertising, "create an image." Ask yourself these questions: (1) What am I trying to communicate? and (2) What is the interviewer trying to communicate?

Obviously, you will want to respond well to questions and to provide pertinent and appropriate information about yourself. But keep in mind that not all the information you convey takes a verbal form. Consciously or not, you communicate important information in the way you present yourself. Your style of dress, tone of voice, inflections, gestures, posture, and other physical signals will express your attitudes and personal picture of yourself to others as loudly and clearly as your words do. Professional interviewers rely heavily on both verbal and nonverbal messages.

Listening, too, is an active function of interpersonal communication. The listener receives and processes new information. A good interview involves more than an "I talk, you listen; you talk, I listen" format. A good listener uses new information in adjusting his or her responses to the dynamic situation. The listener remains involved and in control of in-coming information. Therefore, make a conscious effort to hear everything the interviewer says to you. Attend to the information the interviewer gives about the position, the organization, and about yourself. Do not simply wait for a direct question to come to you or for your "turn" to speak; listen and comprehend.

Construct your own picture of the way this particular organization sees itself from what you learn in the interview. If you are being interviewed at their facilities, make mental notes about how the "front-office people" dress; note the decor and the general working atmosphere. If you are being interviewed away from their offices, the person who is interviewing you is your only source of information. What kind of image does this person project? What is he or she telling you, through direct and indirect messages, about the people you may be working with? How well does the projected image of the organization match your image of yourself? In the best employment situations these images will meld easily with each other.

INTERVIEWING TECHNIQUES

Since the interviewer normally sets the tone of an interview, you should familiarize yourself with some of the most common interviewing techniques. If you are able to recognize the "type" of meeting you are in, you will be better able to (1) predict the general direction of the interview and prepare to introduce specific elements from your personal interview plan, and (2) reduce anxiety, even in an apparently tense situation, by knowing what to expect.

The diagram in Figure 4.2 illustrates the most common elements employed by interviewers to influence the atmosphere of an interview; structure and stress. All interviews are characterized by some combination of these two elements: structure/stress, structure/no stress, no structure/ stress, or no structure/no stress. The diagram emphasizes the fact that these factors are interdependent and rarely fixed.

The following discussion explores the influence of each and offers suggested methods of dealing with them. The student is advised to look for combinations of structure and stress techniques in the interview and adjust his or her responses accordingly.

STRUCTURE

The most obvious device an interviewer may utilize is structure—that is, the interviewer determines the shape and design of the interview by remaining in total control. Ask yourself these questions: How free is this meeting? Will I be allowed to bring items into the discussion easily, at my own discretion, or will most of my time and attention be directed by the interviewer toward responding to specific questions?

An interviewer who wants to keep the meeting tightly structured usually prepares a rather specific set of closed questions and presents it in turn to each person applying for the position. This approach represents the interviewer's attempt to evaluate candidates' knowledge of required information objectively by comparing sets of answers. Therefore, the answers to these questions are normally quite specific. In a structured situation one often gets a feeling that the interviewer is compartmentalizing; when one item is finished he or she moves methodically on to the next. Consequently, the interviewee has little time to ask questions or modify the direction the interviewer has chosen.

If you find yourself in a structured meeting, a degree of special planning is necessary to insure that your own personal interview plan is covered; the more structured the interview is, the more difficult it will be to introduce your own information. It may become apparent that you

FIGURE 4.2. The relationship of
structure and stress.

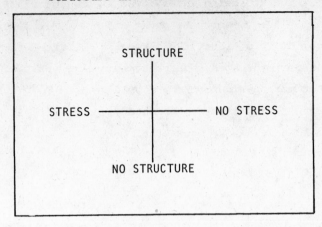

will be given no chance to present your data unless you vie for control. In such an instance, you could wait for a pause or be prepared to insert points toward the end of the meeting, when you may expect to be asked whether you have any questions. A good response would be another question: "Do you want to hear about my special training in . . . ?" If you feel that time is running out, however, a simple, polite, and direct interruption of the interviewer's structure would be most appropriate: "Excuse me, but I feel that there are certain additional things about me that you should know. For instance . . . "

The unstructured interview technique can be just as nerve-wracking for an unprepared applicant. In this situation the interviewer is usually less interested in your answers to predetermined questions than in the modes of thinking by which you arrive at them. This interviewer might also want to determine how you conduct yourself in an unstructured situation. Rather than setting a tone of interrogation, therefore, he usually allows you to set the tone and determine the direction of the conversation. Obviously, this kind of freedom can be extremely worthwhile if it is well-managed. Once again, the fundamental key to success is being able to present your strongest points simply and clearly. Think about your responses carefully; take your time in answering, develop each response completely, and avoid digressions. Refer to your notes if necessary.

Often, in an unstructured situation, the interviewer will ask only open questions, such as, "What are your professional goals?" "Do you see yourself doing this kind of work in ten years?" or simply, "Tell me something about yourself." Be prepared as well for questions based on hypothetical situations. These questions are usually preceded by a "what if" phrase, either stated or implied—for example, "What would you do if . . . ?" or, "How do you think you would react to a problem such as . . . ?"

The particular job at hand may also affect the nature of the questions asked. For example, the hiring decision for a job in a technical field would presumably be based on the candidates' specific knowledge, so closed questions and a structured interview would be appropriate. On the other end of the spectrum, a counselor or social worker interviewing for a job should expect open inquiries related to attitudes about working with people or handling unexpected situations. Ask yourself what kind of information you would need to know about someone you might hire in your own field.

STRESS

Generally, interviewers try to put applicants at ease during a selection interview—even in a structured situation. They realize that the nature of the meeting itself may produce tension and do what they can to reduce it. Only when interviewees are relaxed are they able to think clearly and give their most representative responses to inquiries. Therefore, an interviewer may encourage the applicant to sit back, drink a cup of coffee, and smoke a cigarette. (NOTE: if you smoke, do not do so during the interview without requesting permission). The atmosphere of the meeting is made as casual and unthreatening as possible, and the applicant is encouraged to look upon the interviewer as a friendly person. In this setting the interview can take on the tone of a comfortable conversation, and even though the interviewer may adopt a structured approach, the applicant is given plenty of time to respond.

However, some interviewers pressure applicants to see how they react; they conduct what is called a "stress interview." Proponents of this approach feel that certain jobs require people who respond well under stress; therefore they use the interview situation to test the applicants' tolerance for high-pressure situations. A small number of the interviewers who employ stress techniques feel that applicants reveal certain information in high-stress situations which they would not otherwise express. Stress interviews are not necessarily unfriendly or hostile, but they do put more pressure on applicants to keep their wits about them.

Interviewers usually build stress in two ways: by speeding up the pace and by asking emotionally charged questions. With an increased pace, the interviewer will ask more questions and the applicant will have less time between them to compose answers or to relax. And, if the inquiries themselves are highly personal or difficult to answer, tension is bound to increase in the room. For example, an interviewer might easily disconcert you by asking a series of textbook questions from your professional field. In such an instance you would literally be given an oral examination in your area; you may be asked to define, list, explain, or evaluate difficult material. Or, more dramatically, the interviewer might introduce potentially sensitive questions with little or no preparation:

"You certainly change jobs frequently. Is there a problem there?"

"Would you have difficulty working with a female supervisor?" (If the applicant is male)

"Are you married? Do you plan to have children?" (If the applicant is female)

"Did you know that we generally hire people with more experience than you have?"

Such questions could unnerve anyone. But remember that much of their impact derives from the interview context in which they are asked. Consider how you would answer such questions in a more comfortable situation. Or if you feel that you are being forced into a stress situation, seize control: Request more time in which to formulate your responses, or point out, courteously but straightforwardly, that certain questions are simply not relevant to your job performance. Maintain your composure; keep in mind too that the interviewer may be pushing you to see how you react.

In practice, an interviewer rarely concentrates on structure or stress techniques exclusively. A normal interview is a mixture of approaches that tends toward the center of the diagram. But, by becoming familiar with the extremes you can learn to identify the norm. For instance, if you realize early on that an interviewer is relying on open questions and urging you to talk at length,

93

you can begin to implement your interview plan and ask questions of your own. Conversely, if you feel that the thrust of the meeting is toward closed questions, stress, and controlled structure, you can take advantage of your understanding by planning other stratagems to bring your points in. In other words, without being overtly dominant or overbearing, but by comprehending the intention of the interviewer, you can turn almost any interviewing situation to your own advantage.

THINGS TO BRING TO THE INTERVIEW

Always carry a few extra copies of your resume to employment meetings. This simple precaution protects against unexpected contingencies—the interviewer might forget his or her copy, or more than one person from the organization might be present. Also, bring a copy of the resume for yourself. You can refer to it during the meeting, and, if you should have to fill out a standard employment application (see Appendix B), all the necessary information will be readily available.

The interview is also an excellent opportunity to display examples of your work. Bring proposals, awards, publications, drawings, brochures, evaluations, projects, notebooks, papers, or other items that can be contained in a professional portfolio. (See Chapter 2 under the heading "References and Letters of Recommendation.")

Finally, bring the notes you have made on the company, your personal interview plan, and the questions you wish to ask. Do not be shy about using notes; they reflect your sincere interest in the job. And, by all means, have pen and paper available so that you will be able to take additional notes during the interview if you wish.

CONCLUDING THE INTERVIEW

Many experts feel that the last few moments of an interview are the most crucial, so a few thoughts about conclusions are appropriate. It has been estimated that the final ten percent of the interview has the most critical effect on an interviewer's evaluation. The last impression is at least as important to an applicant as the first.

How, then, can the applicant leave the best last impression? In the most general terms, the best conclusion is one that brings a feeling of completeness or closure to the meeting. Try to summarize the period that has just transpired while synthesizing all the relevant aspects of the job-search process to that moment in time. You might use the opportunity to review the interview, introduce additional information, acknowledge new information, or draw a final conclusion. Your main objective should be to show the interviewer that you have taken the meeting seriously and are able to put it into perspective. Thus, drawing the interview to a conclusion tests your knowledge, sensitivity, awareness, and capacity to analyze concisely.

EVALUATING THE INTERVIEW

Since the interview is part of the overall job-search you will find it useful to keep a record of what occurred there. You will want to add this material to your earlier notes on this specific job. As soon as possible after the meeting, then, write down each of the salient points discussed in the interview; if you took notes, they may only have to be expanded. Pay special attention to what the interviewer said; his or her last words may be quite important here. How eager is the company to fill the position? How negotiable are salary and working conditions?

Or, how soon may you expect a decision? Also try to evaluate the meeting objectively. Were you able to present your qualifications clearly? Do you still consider this a good lead? If so, save these notes and add them to your Mailing Log for use in preparing your follow-up letter.

CHECKLIST FOR THE PERSONAL INTERVIEW

1. Prepare yourself beforehand:

    a. Learn about the company and the job.

        1. Read company literature.

        2. Use the research methods described in Chapter 1.

    b. Know about yourself and your career:

        1. Think about the open questions.

        2. Decide what you have to offer.

    c. Practice answering questions out loud.

2. During the interview act natural and be yourself.

    a. Present essential information about your qualifications.

    b. Answer questions clearly and courteously.

    c. Have supplementary material on hand.

    d. Ask relevant questions.

    e. Take notes if you wish.

    f. Don't try to second-guess answers or bluff.

3. Afterwards evaluate the interview.

    a. Record key points so you won't forget.

    b. Prepare a follow-up letter (see Chapter 5).

EXERCISES

1. Discussion topics

    a. Why are personal interviews normally required?

    b. What kind of information is the interviewer usually looking for?

    c. How should you prepare for an interview?

    d. What information should you seek to learn about an organization before an interview? during? after?

    e. What are the most difficult questions you might have to face? Open? Personal?

    f. How can you prepare for difficult questions? for stress?

    g. What should you bring to an interview?

    h. Who should control the meeting?

    i. Should you answer personal questions? Why? Why not?

    j. What are the advantages of an "open" interview over a "closed" one? disadvantages?

    k. Should you prepare a script for the interview?

2. Using your resume and letter of application, prepare an interview plan for yourself. Note the information, in order of importance, that you want to communicate to the interviewer about yourself and your qualifications.

3. Make a list of the interview questions you would have the most difficulty answering. Consider deficiencies in your background, and any other area of concern where you could be vulnerable in an interview. Invent stressful and open questions that would give you trouble. Study the list at your leisure and prepare possible responses. Take notes.

4. Set up practice interviewing sessions in your class. Enact complete ten-minute sessions from introduction to conclusion. If at all possible, arrange to have strangers conduct the interviews and videotape the proceedings for analysis. Criticize your own tape personally with your instructor. How do you look to others? Which questions gave you difficulty? Identify the strengths and weaknesses of your session. What would you change?

5. Make a list of all of the potential professions represented in your class. Begin with the first; ask each person in the room, in turn, to suggest a different item that an applicant for that job could bring with them to an interview. For example, how many different things could an engineer bring? an accountant? a teacher? Then try this exercise with other professions chosen at random from newspaper classifieds. Take notes when your field is discussed.

6. How is the structure of an interview, with regard to introduction, body, and conclusion, similar to the structure of a letter of application? What are the major differences?

Follow-Ups and Reply Letters 5

The Final Stage

What should I do if they don't call me back?
Can I speed up an employer's decision?
How can I keep the irons hot?
When should I send out a follow-up letter?
Can I bargain for a better salary?
How should I evaluate a job offer?
Suppose I don't want it now?
When is a telephone call more useful than a letter?

This chapter is devoted to those messages required after the applications have been submitted and the job interview has been conducted. It explains when and why certain related letters should be sent, and suggests what their content should be through descriptions, checklists, and examples. For instance, how can the job seeker reestablish contact with an employer after a long silence? And, what is an interview follow-up? When is this device appropriate and what should it contain? This chapter also covers techniques for recording and evaluating information about jobs, and a method to aid the candidate in making decisions.

FOLLOW-UP LETTERS

After the job interview the applicant must endure a waiting period; it is the employer's turn to respond now, and he will not do so until a decision has been made. But if the employer's silence goes on for too long, you may either consider it to be an informal refusal or a signal that you should do something more. When you have waited for an employer's response for more than two weeks, use the follow-up letter as a device to get things moving again. If it is successful it will let the employer know that you are still interested and encourage him to make you an offer. If not, it may lead to a refusal. Though disappointing, the refusal will alleviate doubt, and free you to focus on more promising prospects.

The follow-up letter is appropriate in three situations.

1. As a courteous response to an interview, treated as a routine part of the application process.

2. If you receive no reply within 2 weeks following the submission of an application package.

3. If you receive no response within 14 days after an interview.

The Routine Interview Follow-Up

The first type of follow-up letter is the normal response to the interview itself; it is more of a courteous letter of acknowledgment than a request for a response (see Figure 5.1). The writer thanks the interviewer for the opportunity to speak with him personally and learn more about the position being offered. It is a simple, courteous, and direct message, and it should be sent as a normal part of the application process.

Begin the interview follow-up letter with a sentence or two expressing appreciation for the interview itself. The bulk of the message can contain your personal analysis of the interview. Recount your impressions and the points that particularly interested you in the discussion. Or take this opportunity to introduce new information about your background and experience related to specific questions that may have come up during the meeting. The conclusion of the letter should be positive and reflect goodwill. In brief, the basic components of this letter are:

1. Reference to the interview and expression of thanks.

2. Analysis of interview and any additional application information.

3. Complimentary close; may include oblique reference to status of application.

The overall effect of this letter should be quite positive. The letter should show the reader that you are thorough, courteous, efficient, and sincerely interested in the job. On the personal level, writing this letter allows you to wrap up your application for this position; it is your chance to tie up all of the loose ends neatly.

The Application Follow-Up

The two remaining situations calling for follow-up letters are "no-response situations." These letters will be designed to get things moving again when you suspect, after an extended silence, that communication has broken down. Timing and tone are particularly important in these situations.

The follow-up sent when you have had no response to an application is the most mechanical and simply structured of all the employment-related letters. This is true for two reasons: First, there is basically no new information to be communicated in the letter, and second, you should not invest too much further effort in a lead that is starting to seem questionable. If you receive no response to your follow-up, cross this lead off your list.

Fundamentally, this letter should recapitulate the message in your application letter. The follow-up is comprised of three elements:

1. Reference to the initial letter of application.

2. Recapitulation of the first application.

3. Request for a response.

See Figure 5.2 for a sample of an application follow-up.

FIGURE 5.1. A sample routine interview follow-up letter.

1139 S. Wabash Avenue
Dallas, TX 75229
January 29, 1976

Edward Everett Hadley
Personnel Officer
Continental Map Company
50-60 E. Huron Street
Wheaton, TX 76118

Dear Mr. Hadley:

I appreciated the opportunity to meet with you last week during your visit to Dallas. Thank you for taking the time to discuss with me personally the position of Insurance Officer with Continental Map.

You explained the requirements of the position and working conditions at Continental to me in such a way that I now feel I understand the company's "family loyalty." I can now appreciate, especially after talking with representatives of other companies, your statement that you wouldn't work for anyone else.

Also, you asked if I had experience in computer applications of insurance to small companies. I answered yes, but did not have the opportunity to elaborate. I am, therefore, enclosing a transcript of my last year at the university, with the computer theory and language courses underlined in red pencil.

Talking with you, Mr. Hadley, has made me even more eager to obtain a position with Continental. Thank you once more, and I hope to hear from you soon.

Sincerely yours,

Dale K. Edwards

Dale K. Edwards

FIGURE 5.2. A sample application follow-up letter.

156 N. Aqueduct Drive
Salt Lake City, UT 84102
July 7, 1976

Claude D. Owens
Manager
Chino Excavators
909 N. Redwood Road
Salt Lake City, UT 84104

Dear Mr. Owens:

A few weeks ago I sent you my resume and application for the position of a
lead surveyor with your organization. I hope it has not been misplaced,
for I have not received a reply from you.

If you will take a few minutes, Mr. Owens, to review my qualifications, I
believe you will see that I am a conscientious and experienced surveyor.
I have the equivalent of a college degree in civil engineering, plus four-
teen years experience with local Utah contractors.

I hope that you have a place for another good surveyor now; if not, please
keep my resume on file and feel free to call me in the future if anything
opens up. As I stated in my earlier letter, I am available any afternoon
after 4:00 to come to your office for an interview.

Please let me hear from you soon.

Sincerely,

Jack Meras

Jack Meras

THE NO-RESPONSE INTERVIEW FOLLOW-UP

The follow-up letter required when there is no response to an interview—or to your first follow-up—is the most subtle of the follow-up letters. It is normally employed for two reasons: either the company that interviewed you is painfully slow in making their decision, or you have other offers pending and you want to hurry the decision along. You may or may not mention the latter in your letter depending upon the nature of the negotiations at the time.

Begin the letter with a reference to the interview. Do not emphasize gratitude, though; the tone of this message should be more formal. The body of the letter should be a clear and precise statement of the reasons why you require a response at this time. You may refer to your sense of the interview's success, mentioning statements that were made or conclusions you drew. You may also bring in pertinent new information. But do not try to use this letter to negotiate; instead, emphasize your desire to hear from the employer. Conclude with a request for action—either a firm decision or information on the status of your application. In summary, this follow-up should be comprised of these elements:

1. Courteous opening; may include a reference to the interview.
2. Reason for request; may include analysis of interview or additional information.
3. Request for action: either an immediate decision or information on status of application.
4. Complimentary close.

On the surface this follow-up letter may seem aggressive; in reality, if it is written with care, it will start communication rolling again and bring you the information you need to make a decision. See Figure 5.3 for a sample.

THE MAILING LOG

Always keep accurate records of everything you send out, particularly if you are mailing a number of applications at once. A systematic follow-up program is essential in a successful employment campaign. This effort, in turn, is dependent on your care in recording your messages and replies. If you are only applying to a few companies, a simple date file containing carbon or photocopies of your correspondence plus the replies received is sufficient. But if you decide to blanket the field with applications, more extensive records are necessary. The mailing log in Figure 5.4 illustrates the kinds of information you need and the advantages of recording it all together in one place. You can keep track of all incoming and outgoing correspondence *and* check the intervals between them regularly. Then, when the time lapse between stages lasts too long, you can send a follow-up as a matter of course. Establish your own schedule concerning follow-up messages—two weeks is usually about right—and send them out automatically when the need becomes apparent on the mailing log.

The telephone can be an extremely valuable aid in the job-search process. The advantages and disadvantages of phone contact can be summed up quickly: it is more informal and impersonal than a letter or an interview, but it is much faster. It can be used effectively at all levels of the employment campaign: to look for leads, to set up appointments, and as a follow-up technique.

If you use the telephone, however, remember that you will have no record of what has been said unless you take notes. Do not rely on your memory. Prepare a set of sheets, similar in layout to the mailing log, and use them to remind yourself what has been said. Pay particular attention to

FIGURE 5.3. A sample no-response interview follow-up.

16 Sunside Avenue
Washington, DC 20004
July 12, 1975

Dr. Erich Easter
Personnel Director
Ironwood Fireman's Fund
Suite 321
1010 Maine Avenue
Washington, DC 20005

Dear Dr. Easter:

This is a difficult letter for me to write. I hope you will appreciate that I am motivated by special circumstances, and would normally not make this kind of a request of a potential employer.

Following our interview last week, I decided that, if possible, I would like to become an employee of Ironwood Fireman's Fund. Unfortunately, though, I had already interviewed with a number of other firms in the field. One of them, Crestway Limited, has recently sent me a quite nice offer. My dilemma now is whether or not to accept. If I am a serious candidate for the position with Ironwood, I will of course notify Crestway that I will not be available.

Could I possibly hear from you this week concerning the status of my application? I do not wish to rush you in your decision, or ask you to betray a professional confidence but, as you see, I am in a quandary because of my lack of information.

Thank you for your assistance.

Yours truly,

Edward Edgar De La Torre

Edward Edgar De La Torre

FIGURE 5.4. Sample Mailing Log Sheet

COMPANY	CONTACT	FOLLOW-UP	RESPONSE	NOTES
Tellalite	Application/Resume (9/7)	Send in January	No (9/17)	No openings now. They will keep application on file until March. Contact again in late January.
Actuex	Inquiry (9/10)		No (9/18)	No hiring in immediate future. Still a good company to work for. Contact again in about a year.
Littype	Inquiry (9/6)	Follow-up Letter (10/6)		If no response by 12/6 drop any further inquiries.
Tridee	Inquiry (9/12)	Application/Resume (9/19)	Maybe (9/18)	Sent job description (9/18). May be hiring in December. Send out complete package now.
Rocketyke	Application/Resume (9/7)		Yes (9/12)	Interview 9/17, 3:00 p.m. Research company more fully prior to interview.
All Brite	Resume only (9/15)			

names (ask for correct spelling if in doubt), telephone numbers, appointment times, and other specific data, and jot down your general impressions after a telephone conversation to help you sort out your attitudes. Avoid making commitments over the telephone without arranging for a subsequent letter of confirmation. Always have important items in writing. If the lead looks good, be sure to follow it up in writing and include your application package.

REPLY LETTERS

If your job campaign has been fruitful, you will begin receiving employment offers after the personal interviews. At this stage you must be prepared to compose the last type of job-related letter, the reply. You must let the employer know as soon as possible whether you accept the offer. Later in this chapter the actual decision-making process will be discussed. For the moment we will consider the actual composition of reply letters expressing (1) acceptance, (2) refusal, (3) a request for further negotiation.

THE ACCEPTANCE LETTER

An acceptance is one of the most pleasant letters to write (see Figure 5.5). Once again, a statement of appreciation makes a fine beginning; it can be coupled with your acceptance easily. "Thank you, I am pleased to accept your offer. . . . " The body of your letter—if the personnel officer has done her work well and sent you a written job offer with a clear statement of the conditions of employment—briefly reaffirms the offer. But if elements of the offer were not clearly stated, request clarification in your acceptance letter, and state explicitly what you are agreeing to. This is particularly important if critical items are not mentioned in the offer letter, or remain vague, as often happens if the offer is made verbally. Your acceptance letter may also include information or instructions you have relating to the employment. For example,

> Please arrange with your insurance person to start my health and major medical insurance plans as soon as it is convenient.

The acceptance letter may be quite brief if everything in the offer meets with your satisfaction. But if you have any questions or reservations or foresee possible disagreement in the future, make this letter as long as necessary to alleviate all problems now. This is the time for *complete* accord. Use the acceptance letter to assure it.

To summarize, the major elements in the acceptance letter are:

1. Appreciation for the offer.
2. Statement of acceptance.
3. Brief reaffirmation of employment conditions, or your statement of employment conditions.
4. Any instructions based on employment or notices.
5. Complimentary close.

FIGURE 5.5. A sample acceptance letter.

77 S. Gibbs Street
Gatewood, KY 40486
July 17, 1976

Mr. Cecil Sheldon
Personnel Manager
Jane Pruett Beauty Spas
77-89 E. Bonnie Brea Road
Lexington, KY 40506

Dear Mr. Sheldon:

I am quite pleased to accept your company's kind offer for my services.
I have read the terms specified in your letter carefully and I concur with
all of them as stated.

I do have a favor to ask you, though, Mr. Sheldon. Due to moving expenses
that will be required in coming down to Lexington, I would appreciate it if
you could arrange for my first check to be available on August 3. I realize
that you may have a policy of not preparing new employee's checks for a short
week—only three days in this case—but this is a one-time request that grows
out of an unusual circumstance. I do hope that you can make this arrangement
for me.

Thank you again for this offer. I am looking forward to beginning my new
job with Jane Pruett next month, and I am confident that it will be a mutu-
ally rewarding relationship.

Sincerely,

Richard Washington
Richard Washington

The Letter of Refusal

Preparing a letter refusing an offer of employment may not seem too difficult. At times, it might even seem unnecessary, but a polite refusal is an applicant's responsibility as well as a professional courtesy. It notifies the employer that you are not interested in working for the company, and thereby allows him to continue the search with the least delay (see Figure 5.6). Also, it makes good sense, in terms of the future, to end negotiations pleasantly on a note of goodwill. The keys to a successful refusal letter are tact and tone.

Begin with a word of gratitude for the offer itself, and lead from this into the negative reply: "I appreciate your considering me for this position, but I am unable to accept your offer." Make the statement clear and definite; do not attempt to be coy and leave the reader with the impression that you are still fishing. If the employers want to respond again, that is their choice; do not plan on it, though, after you send this letter. By the same token, the message of refusal should not seem too abrupt. The body of the letter should briefly explain why you are refusing the job. This explanation could be a real service to the employer. You may wish to be purposefully vague about the reasons for your decision, but if you give an employer no solid feedback, how will he know what went wrong? If, for example, the salary he offered was too low, he may never raise it unless he receives several refusals stating that the salary was unacceptable. Finally, conclude the letter with a simple statement of goodwill. To summarize, the refusal letter should include the following:

1. Appreciation for the offer.
2. Statement of refusal.
3. Explanation of reasons.
4. Goodwill close.

Do not put off writing refusal letters. They are not crucial to you personally, but they are important to the employer and to others who may be under consideration for the position you are refusing. The sooner you step out of the way, the easier it will be for others.

Another letter, closely allied to the refusal letter in tone and structure, is used to end the application process. If you find a position, it is a good idea to send out letters to everyone you have already contacted, including employment agencies, notifying them that you are no longer available. Prepare this letter in the same manner you would a refusal, but thank the recipient for considering your application.

The Request for Further Negotiation

The final letter to be considered opens or continues negotiation after a job offer has been made. This letter is similar to both the acceptance and the refusal, except that it has an added "if" clause. That is, the applicant agrees to consider the offer only if certain changes in compensation or working conditions are discussed further (see Figure 5.7).

Either party can instigate negotiations concerning salary or other benefits. Do not be reluctant to ask for adjustments in the offer if you are sure your request is fair. But assess the situation first to determine whether your request will cost you the job—some employers simply will not want you badly enough to compromise. Once you have decided to bargain, though, carefully weigh your bargaining power—that is, consider how badly the employer wants to hire you—and do not

FIGURE 5.6. A sample letter of refusal.

674 Cook Drive
Honolulu, HI 96814
August 30, 1976

Mr. Leslie Howe
President
Howe & Howe Importers
77 Ward Avenue
Honolulu, HI 96817

Dear Mr. Howe:

I received your offer for a position with Howe & Howe as marketing analyst this morning. I truly appreciate the generous terms and kind words concerning my qualifications. Unfortunately, though, I have decided, with all due respect to your company to refuse the offer.

Recently I have been carrying on discussions with another firm in the Honolulu area for my services, and this week they offered me a position. Their terms were consistent with the offer you made, but I will have a greater chance for advancement with them; in fact we have discussed my becoming a member of the Tokyo branch immediately.

I am sure that you will appreciate my desire to work for a company that offers me this kind of opportunity.

I am sorry that I cannot become an employee of Howe & Howe at this time. I hope I will be able to meet with you again in the future. Until that time, aloha!

Virginia Young
Virginia Young

FIGURE 5.7. A sample request for further negotiation.

43 Burnside Avenue
Atlanta, GA 30323
June 17, 1976

Ms. Sarah Hafner
Personnel Officer
Alwell Hospital Supplies
180 Commerce Drive NW
Atlanta, GA 30318

Dear Ms. Hafner:

Thank you for your recent employment offer. I am sincerely interested in becoming the administrative assistant to Mr. Alonzo, your Western District Manager, but I would like the opportunity to clarify two items with you before I accept.

The letter I received on Wednesday did not mention that Alwell would reimburse me for relocating my family in Phoenix, and the salary figure quoted was not comparable to my present earnings as an executive secretary with Structure Systems Research. As I recall, we discussed both of these points at our interview last week. Could I have misunderstood?

If it is convenient, I would appreciate the opportunity of meeting with you again next week. I will call your secretary on Monday to make an appointment.

I am looking forward to seeing you next week—and to beginning work with Alwell in the near future.

Sincerely,

Robert Decker

Robert Decker

become emotional about winning your point. Stay cool and be objective. Remember that the employment situation may involve both a buyers' and a sellers' market. Ask yourself how difficult it would be for the employer to find someone else for this position. How unique are your qualifications? How much leverage do you really have in this situation? At what point will the employer decide that you are asking for more than he is willing to pay?

Once you have made your decision to bargain, your letter requesting further negotiation should begin with a normal thank-you for the offer and then move quickly into either a request for further discussion or a conditional statement. Pay close attention to these sentences; they should express both a request *and* a willingness to negotiate:

> I appreciate your recent offer. I read it with a great deal of enthusiasm, and would like to accept now; however . . .
>
> I am sincerely interested in becoming an Alwell employee, but first I would like the opportunity of discussing the quoted salary with you.
>
> Thank you for your recent employment offer; it was most generous. Unfortunately, though, I still feel that one or two small items need further clarification before I can accept.
>
> I thank you for your offer, but at this time there are still some unresolved conditions that we must discuss further.

You should strive to set a tone of courtesy and openness from the beginning. The "at this time," "however," or "but" should appear to refer to a temporary condition that can easily be resolved through discussion. The pivotal element in the bargaining process is your willingness to accept the offer; this willingness itself should seem to lead the discussion naturally into specific points.

The body of the negotiation letter addresses itself to the items you feel are still unresolved, or a request for a meeting to discuss them further. If you do desire a conference, do not include your arguments in the letter, but identify the items you wish to discuss. The letter can then serve as an agenda for the negotiation meeting. Know what you want, and ask for it. If your requests appear unreasonable or vague, or if you just seem to be holding out on the chance that the offer will improve, the hiring agent will probably respond with "Take it or leave it."

You might suggest a compromise between previously disputed points in the body of the letter, though this is not the best method of bargaining, especially at the beginning. Rather, try to explain your point of view so that a compromise is implied which can be initiated by the employer. Only offer a compromise yourself if things have reached a definite impasse. Conclude this letter with a standard goodwill close and the suggestion that the reader respond with his or her thinking on the issue.

Negotiations may continue over an extended period of time, so more than one of these letters may be required. Do not become discouraged if an employer does not meet your requests immediately. Read any replies carefully and decide whether the employer has really refused your conditions adamantly. If there still seems to be a solid area for bargaining—that is, if you received less than a patent no—take an aggressive posture and try again. But you may find no desire to bargain communicated in the response. Then it is probably time to simply take the offer as it stands or refuse it. Always keep the tone of your negotiation fair and open; never insist and avoid issuing ultimatums.

In summary the separate elements of the negotiation letter are:

1. Appreciation of the offer.

2. Statement of nonacceptance followed by the "but" or "unless" clause.

3. Summary of negotiable items.

4. Your reasons or request for a meeting.

5. Optional: your counteroffer.

6. Request for response.

7. Goodwill close.

THE FINAL DECISION

Sooner or later in your career you will have to sit down and decide whether you want to accept a particular job offer. Such decisions can be overwhelming unless you have sincerely assessed your own background and career goals, and then compared the potential of available jobs with your own personal goals and requirements (see Chapter 1). If the match is close, your decision to accept a job will probably be automatic. If the match is poor, you will have to consider other alternatives: refuse the position outright, attempt to negotiate further, or accept on an interim basis—that is, go to work for a limited period of time while you continue to search for a better prospect. But even deciding on these options can be difficult unless you have done your homework about the company in question.

The following list shows a sampling of items related to employee benefits, compensations, and working conditions which a careful job seeker might investigate before deciding to accept a job. If you are considering a job offer, make a list of the elements that are most important to you and find out how well the organization in question compares on these matters with others in the field. Remember, this list is only an example; it may not necessarily relate to your situation or reflect your interests. What are your personal priorities? The time to make a decision in terms of yourself is *before* you accept a job. Which conditions of employment are most important to you?

1. Initial salary and raise schedule
2. Sick leave payment
3. Separation allowance (severance pay)
4. Old-age, survivors, disability, and health insurance
5. Travel and per diem compensation
6. Workers' compensation
7. Bonuses, commissions, and other compensations
8. Credit union
9. Union affiliations
10. Service awards
11. Chances for advancement
12. Company-paid education programs
13. Paid holidays
14. Unemployment compensation
15. Management incentives
16. Special clothing allowances
17. Necessity to relocate
18. Pension plans
19. Special company training programs
20. Paid vacations

21. Reimbursement for moving
22. Potential for advancement within company
23. Job safety record
24. Travel requirements
25. Purchasing discounts for employees
26. Suggestion bonuses
27. Size of company
28. Major health plans
29. Tax-sheltered annuity
30. Number of supervisors

31. Overtime requirements and pay
32. Degree of privacy
33. Profit-sharing program
34. Employee thrift plan
35. Degree of independence
36. Retirement plan
37. Job security
38. Geographic location
39. Amount of travel required
40. Patent or publication rights

If you have an analytical nature, you may want to use a Decision/Analysis Chart (DAC) in evaluating a job offer (see Figure 5.8). Begin by listing the benefits you consider most crucial—ten or twelve should be sufficient. Then rate them, in terms of each company you have applied to, on a scale of one to five. Finally—and this step is the key to the success and objectivity of this method—write down your reason for awarding that particular rating. When the chart is complete, add up the points you awarded the company and use the resulting index number to compare various companies' offers. Be sure to compare the same items in each situation. You can also use this approach when you are considering leaving a current job and want to weigh the alternatives.

One final word about decision making: Don't panic. Consider all the options open to you before making a final choice—try not to feel pressured into a premature decision. In other words, do not grab the first job offer you receive unless you are completely satisfied. You should sincerely believe that the offer you accept is better than subsequent offers you might receive, and you should be able to support that belief with objective information. Therefore, it is a good idea to hold an offer for a few days without responding either way while you continue to interview with other companies. Gather information in these later interviews so you can actively compare the job under consideration with the job you have been offered.

EXERCISES

1. Discussion topics
   a. What should you do if a company does not contact you after an interview?
   b. How long should you wait patiently?
   c. Is it possible to speed up an employer's decision?
   d. How many kinds of follow-up messages are there? What are they?
   e. What employment considerations are most important to you? salary? fringe benefits? others?
   f. What is the value of a mailing log? ADC?
   g. What are the advantages and disadvantages of using the telephone?
   h. Why bother to send a refusal letter?
   i. How aggressive should you be during negotiations?
   j. Is one follow-up letter sufficient?
   k. Why is it important to give reasons to yourself when using the Decision/Analysis technique?

FIGURE 5.8. Sample Decision/Analysis Chart (DAC)

TRIDEE CORPORATION	RATINGS					SALES REPRESENTATIVE
EMPLOYEE BENEFITS, WORKING CONDITIONS, AND POTENTIAL GROWTH	POOR	FAIR	GOOD	EXCEL-LENT	SUPE-RIOR	REASONS FOR RATINGS
Salary			3			Straight salary. No commissions. Annual bonus (3 percent). Raises on merit only.
Encouragement toward advanced degree					5	Paid in full by company.
Life and medical insurance		2				50 percent, on a matching basis.
Relocation compensation	1					Would have to move (400 miles). No reimbursement.
Vacation				4		Two weeks paid annually—on a staggered basis. Company will give bonus for work.
Holidays			3			7 per year—paid.
Travel				4		Paid travel and per diem. No expense accounts.
Potential for advancement					5	Policy of promoting from within. Most managers are over 50 now.
Sick leave			3			1 paid day per month. No reimbursement plan.
TOTAL	1	2	9	8	10	30

2. Write a personal follow-up letter for an interview.

3. Assume that you have been working for Allied Units for two years, and now you have decided to begin looking for another position with a greater opportunity for advancement. Assume you wrote the letter in Figure 5.6 to a company two years ago. Write a letter to this company to reopen communication and begin the job-search process again.

4. You have decided to accept a position with Griffith Applicances and have just sent them a standard acceptance letter. Unexpectedly, in the next mail, you receive an offer from Goncourt Industries (Goncourt had been number one on your list of preferences, but you had heard nothing from them—even after you sent them a pointed letter of inquiry). You now want to go to work for Goncourt, even though their offer is slightly lower than Griffith's. Write two letters, one to each company, reflecting your new decision.

5. Your employment campaign is just about over; you have been offered two positions, one with Rococo Associates and the other with Necessity Limited. Applying the Decision/Analysis method to the information in the table on the next page, decide which job you would accept. Keep in mind that your rating system will reflect your personal opinions. Compare your reasons for selection with others in the class. Discuss each item individually.

6. When you have made your choice between Rococo and Necessity, assume that you really want to work for the other company. Write a letter negotiating an improved offer from the latter organization.

EXERCISES 5 and 6. Comparing job offers.

BENEFITS	ROCOCO ASSOCIATES	NECESSITY LIMITED
Starting salary	$210 per week	$960 per month
Raise schedule	5% annually (automatic)	2 to 10% biannual review (merit only)
Commissions	20% initial sale	1% duration of contract
Bonuses	1% gross annual salary	none
Holidays	5 annually paid 2 personal unpaid	6 annually paid
Sick leave	Unpaid by Employer: low-rate company insurance available	One day paid per month; cumulative after first six months
Health and life insurance	Low cost: shared	Low cost: shared
Travel required	Moderate: in state	Extensive: local
Supervisors	One Supervisor	Four co-equal department heads
Advancement	Good	Moderate to good
Union affiliation	Required	Not required
Education program	Company pays 5% of approved study	No reimbursement
Location	20 miles from home: automobile required	4 miles from home: public transportation available
Automobile	Company furnished. Company insured.	Contract reimbursement: 15¢ per mile. Personal insurance required.

Appendix

THE COVER LETTER AND RESUME

HAROLD D. JANES

Late last year, the Personnel Management class at the University of Alabama conducted a survey of many of the large corporations listed in the *Fortune Directory* of the 500 largest U.S. corporations in regard to the cover letter and resume of prospective college graduates. The following highlights of the survey summary are presented through the courtesy of *Harold J. Janes*, Professor of Management in the University's School of Commerce and Business Administration.

I. Of the companies responding to the question of preference regarding the intial contact in writing:

> 98% preferred both cover letter and resume
>
> 2% preferred the resume only
>
> 0% preferred the cover letter only

When a cover letter was preferred, the preference was:

> 67% typewritten
>
> 15% handwritten
>
> 13% no preference
>
> 5% mimeographed

II. Ranked by percent response, the companies preferred the following information included in the resume:

> 98% Military status and/or draft classification
>
> 92% Personal information (date of birth, phone, address, marital status, dependents, etc.)
>
> 91% Special interests such as accounting, personnel, sales, statistics, finance, economics

87% General as well as specific educational qualifications such as majors, minors, degree

86% Willingness to relocate (or lack of willingness)

86% A list of scholarships, awards, honors

82% Previous work experience including jobs held, dates of employment, company address, reason for leaving

80% Physical or health status

76% Social data such as fraternities, athletics, clubs, sororities (The respondents to this statement all requested names of the clubs and organizations as well as any offices held.)

57% Salary requirements

57% Major source of financing while in college

48% High school attended, including class rank and date of graduation

46% A list of grades in major and minor subjects (in college)

41% Special aptitudes such as typing, dictation, computers

33% References required as a part of the resume

32% Photograph (not required since it is against the law, but they would have no objections to including a photo)

26% A complete transcript of college grades, attached as a part of the resume

21% General educational qualifications *only*, such as degree, date of graduation (It should be noted that 87% preferred general as well as specific educational qualifications.)

III. Concerning the question, "Do you prefer any restrictions on the length of the resume?":

35% Prefer one page; not more than two

30% One page only

13% Prefer two pages

8% Brief but complete

8% No restrictions

2% Prefer two or three pages

2% Maximum of four pages

2% The more information we have the better chance we have of matching interests with our openings.

IV. In response to the "open end" question, "What should the cover letter include?":

1. The letter should be short, and if the person has a particular reason for his or her interest in our company, it should be clearly stated. Also, indicate when you would be available for an interview. Include your phone number.

2. The letter should include your specific areas of interest, availability, and any requests for information from the company.

3. Omit the "soft soap," indicate your area of interest, your objectives, and any geographical location preference.

4. Just tell us how you learned about the company, why you are contacting us, and what you are looking for.

5. Use the letter to amplify your resume. For example, reasons for low grades or selection of a specific location, etc. Explain any special circumstances in your letter.

6. The letter is an opportunity to be somewhat creative. We see too many stereotyped letters.

V. General Comments and suggestions included:

1. Complete information gives the employer the chance to make an informal judgment and saves time for both the applicant and the company.

2. The cover letter should indicate a special interest in our company; however, receiving a "run of the mill" resume and letter gives the impression that the applicant distributed these indiscriminately like baiting a hook and hoping that some kind of fish will bite.

3. We receive over 200 application letters a day, on the average. Neatness and clarity are essential. Too many letters follow a "canned" professional format. An honest, forthright, individual approach is not only effective, it is *refreshing*.

4. The student should familiarize himself with our company through our annual report, as well as other published information in the *Wall Street Journal*, etc.

5. The cover letter and resume should be viewed as an introduction. It need not be overly "dull." It does not have to tell the total over-all comprehensive story.

Appendix B

SAMPLE APPLICATION FORMS

The following samples of standard employment applications have been included here so that readers can familiarize themselves with the basic information normally required at the time of hiring. The forms have been reproduced by permission.

BANK OF AMERICA
AN EQUAL OPPORTUNITY EMPLOYER

APPLICATION FOR EMPLOYMENT

**ALL APPLICANTS WILL RECEIVE CONSIDERATION FOR EMPLOYMENT WITHOUT REGARD
TO RACE, COLOR, RELIGION, SEX, AGE (40-65), NATIONAL ORIGIN, OR HANDICAP.**

PLEASE USE INK:

NAME	Last	First	Middle	OTHER OR FORMER NAME	SOCIAL SECURITY NO.
PRESENT ADDRESS	Street	City	State	Zip Code	HOW LONG?	Area Code TELEPHONE NO. Number

POSITION OBJECTIVE:

POSITION DESIRED	SALARY EXPECTED $ /Month	DATE AVAILABLE FOR EMPLOYMENT

STATUS DESIRED ☐ Full Time ☐ Other	SHIFT DESIRED	Check One ☐ Day ☐ Swing ☐ Mid.	REFERRED BY:

HAVE YOU PREVIOUSLY APPLIED TO THE BANK OF AMERICA? ☐ No ☐ Yes, at _____ CITY/OFFICE _____ DATE

GENERAL INFORMATION:

U.S. MILITARY SERVICE Branch of Service	Dates of Active Service From To	IF OTHER THAN HONORABLE DISCHARGE, EXPLAIN CIRCUMSTANCES:

HAVE YOU EVER BEEN CONVICTED OF ANYTHING OTHER THAN A MINOR TRAFFIC OFFENSE? ☐ No ☐ Yes ☐ I Don't Know | If "YES" or "I DON'T KNOW", give dates and circumstances:

HAVE YOU EVER BEEN REFUSED FIDELITY BOND? ☐ No ☐ Yes | HAVE YOU EVER FILED BANKRUPTCY? ☐ No ☐ Yes — Schedule A will be required.

ARE YOU CURRENTLY INVOLVED IN THE OPERATIONS OF ANY OTHER BUSINESS? ☐ No ☐ Yes — Give Circumstances:

IF HIRED, CAN YOU FURNISH: Proof of Age? ☐ No ☐ Yes	Proof of Citizenship, Permanent Residency, or Authorization to Work? ☐ No ☐ Yes	DO YOU HAVE ANY RELATIVES EMPLOYED BY BANK OF AMERICA? ☐ Yes ☐ No	FULL NAME	OFFICE/DEPT.

HEALTH: Do you have any condition, illness, or disability, either temporary or permanent, which may affect your ability to do the work in the position applied for?
☐ No ☐ Yes — Specify: _____

EMPLOYMENT AND EDUCATIONAL EXPERIENCE:

DO YOU HAVE ANY QUALIFICATIONS THAT YOU FEEL ARE APPLICABLE FOR THE POSITION APPLIED FOR? ☐ No ☐ Yes		
Educational Background	Highest Level Attained	Employment Experience (give specific dates)

HAVE YOU EVER BEEN EMPLOYED BY BANK OF AMERICA? ☐ No ☐ Yes — Indicate where and when (give specific dates):

HAVE YOU EVER BEEN INVOLUNTARILY DISCHARGED OR FIRED? ☐ No ☐ Yes — Explain circumstances:

I hereby certify that the information provided on this application is accurate to the best of my knowledge and subject to verification by Bank of America. I understand that proof of citizenship, proof of age, and finger printing will be required upon employment. Criminal conviction records must be reviewed before an offer of employment is made. I understand that any misrepresentation or omission of a material fact on my application may be justification for refusal, or if employed, separation from Bank of America employment.

_____ DATE _____ APPLICANT'S SIGNATURE

EXEC-1 2-76 (REV.) ORIGINAL — To Personel Information Center #3618

APPLICATION FOR EMPLOYMENT
OLYMPIA BREWING COMPANY
P. O. Box 947, Olympia, Washington

This application is quite lengthy and purposefully goes into detail in order that we might become better acquainted. All information will be treated confidentially.

Date................................

Position applied for.. Salary Expected................................

Will you accept: Temporary Work.................................... Shift Work.................... Shift Preference....................

Have you been employed by us?.................... Have you ever filed previous application with us?....................

Print or type name.. Home telephone number....................

Present Address..How long have you lived there?....................
No.   Street   City   State

Age .... Date of birth ....
Social Security No. ....
Citizen of U.S.A. or do you have a visa permitting you to work in the U.S.?
Yes ☐   No ☐

Why did you apply at this Company? ....
....
Own Accord .... Agency (Name of Agency) ....
Employee Referral, (Employee Name) ....
Advertisement .... Other ....

Names of relatives employed by this Company..

In case of emergency notify..

EDUCATION

Type of School	Name & Location of School	Dates Attended	Graduate Degrees Received	Courses Majored In	Grade Average
Elementary			☐ Yes ☐ No		
High School			☐ Yes ☐ No		
College					
Graduate School					
Business or Trade School					
Other					

EXTRA CURRICULAR ACTIVITIES (Athletics, Clubs, Etc.)

In high school....................

In college....................

Offices held....................

Offices held....................

Principal source of spending money while in high school and college....................

Part of college expenses you earned ☐ None   ☐ 0-25%   ☐ 25-50%   ☐ 50-75%   ☐ More than 75%

Beginning with the most recent, list below the names and addresses of all your employers.	Time Employed				Kind of Business	Nature of
	FROM		TO			
	Mo.	Yr.	Mo.	Yr.		

Approximate time lost in past two years because of illness_____ Reasons_____

Are you employed at present? _____ If offered a position, how soon could you report for work? _____

References (Not former employers or relatives)	Address	Occupation	Years Known

Draft classification_____ Veteran of Armed Forces?_____

Which Force?_____ Dates of Service_____ _____

Rank at entry_____Rank at discharge_____

Special training received in service_____

_____

Explain present reserve status or commitment_____

ITARY SERVICE RECORD

Work at Start	Salary at Start	Nature of Work At Leaving	Salary at Leaving	Reasons for Leaving	Name of Immediate Supervisor
					Name
					Title
					Name
					Title
					Name
					Title
					Name
					Title
					Name
					Title
					Name
					Title
					Name
					Title
					Name
					Title
					Name
					Title

PERSONAL

Number of brothers_____ Number of sisters_____

Amount of income other than salary: Pension_____ Disability_____ Investment_____ Other_____

What debts or financial obligations do you have at present?_____

_____

Do you carry life insurance outside your present employment? ☐ No ☐ Yes; Amount $_____

Any physical, mental or sensory limitations to assist us in placement? Yes ☐ , No ☐ Please Describe _____

_____

_____

Do you own a car?_____ Do you have full time access to a car?_____

Avocations or hobbies_____

Membership (Clubs, civic, business, professional. Do not include racial, religious or nationality groups)_____

_____

_____

What jobs have you held that gave you the greatest satisfaction? (Please explain.)

_____

_____

_____

Include on the lines below any additional information relative to your interests, qualifications, objectives or reasons for desiring employment with this Company:

_____

_____

_____

CLERICAL

Indicate if experienced in the following:

1. Typewriter _____wpm
2. Shorthand _____wpm
3. Dictaphone _____
4. Teletype _____wpm
5. Vari-type _____wpm

6. Calculator _____
7. IBM Keypunch_____
8. PBX _____
9. MTST _____
10. Addressograph _____

Indicate months of actual office experience:

Type	Time
1. Stenography	_____
2. Bookkeeping	_____
3. IBM Keypunch	_____
4. Other	_____

MAINTENANCE
(to be completed by those applying for maintenance positions only)

Trade or skill_____ Years of experience as apprentice_____ Journeyman_____

Journeyman rating?_____ Date issued_____ Other licenses?_____

What formal vocational training have you taken?_____

Give a brief description of your experience, including types of equipment used:_____

_____

I hereby certify that the answers given by me to the foregoing questions and statements made are true and correct. I agree to submit to physical examination. I also authorize my former employers to give any information they may have regarding me, whether or not it is on their record. I hereby release them and their company from all liability for any damage whatsoever for issuing same. I also authorize an inquiry as to my credit record with the understanding that such information be made available to me upon request. If, upon investigation, anything contained in this application is found to be untrue, or if I do not pass the physical examination, I understand I will not be qualified for employment.

Date_____

_____
Signature of Applicant

Interview by_____ Classification_____ Date_____

Remarks: _____

_____

_____

_____

PROFESSIONAL
EMPLOYMENT APPLICATION

LOCKHEED AIRCRAFT CORPORATION

AN EQUAL OPPORTUNITY EMPLOYER

LOCKHEED-CALIFORNIA COMPANY
P.O. Box 551
Burbank, Calif. 91520

L-1011 TriStar Commercial Jetliners
Military Fixed Wing and Rotary Wing Aircraft
Land Based and Carrier Based Antisubmarine Aircraft
Aerospace and Oceanography Research

LOCKHEED-GEORGIA COMPANY
Marietta, Ga. 30063

Military and Commercial Airlifters
Business Jets
Short Takeoff Research and Design
Aerospace Research

LOCKHEED MISSILES & SPACE COMPANY, INC.
P.O. Box 504
Sunnyvale, Calif. 94088

Strategic Missile Systems
Military and Commercial Space Systems
Communication Satellites
Ground Vehicles
Deep Submersible Vehicles and Systems

LOCKHEED INTERNATIONAL COMPANY
P.O. Box 551
Burbank, Calif. 91520

International Joint Ventures
Foreign Licensing Programs
Overseas Manufacturing Facilities

LOCKHEED AIRCRAFT SERVICE COMPANY
P.O. Box 33
Ontario, Calif. 91764

Aircraft Maintenance. Training Devices.
Electronic and Marine Products and Services
Vehicle Development. Data Recording and
Analysis Systems. Electro-Chemical and
Electro-Mechanical Products

LOCKHEED AIR TERMINAL, INC.
2627 N. Hollywood Way
Burbank, Calif. 91505

Airport Management
Aircraft Fuel Handling
General Aviation Services

LOCKHEED ELECTRONICS COMPANY
U.S. Highway 22
Plainfield, N.J. 07061

Military and Commercial Electronic Systems
Spacecraft and Commercial Instrumentation
Recorders. Computer Memory Systems
and Components. Space Engineering,
Scientific and Technical Support

LOCKHEED PROPULSION COMPANY
P.O. Box 111
Redlands, Calif. 92374

Attack Missile Motors. Solid, Hybrid
and Restartable Pulse Motors.
Launch Escape Motors
Reactor Components. Testing Services

LOCKHEED SHIPBUILDING AND CONSTRUCTION COMPANY
2929 16th Avenue, S.W.
Seattle, Wash. 98134

Shipbuilding, Conversion and Repair
Heavy Construction. Quarry Management
Industrial Cranes and Materials Handling
Equipment

Type or print (in Ink)

APPLICANT'S NAME   Last   First   Middle   DATE PREPARED

CURRENT ADDRESS – No. and Street   HOME PHONE (/ Area Code)

City, State and Zip Code   BUSINESS PHONE (/ Area Code)   EXT.

PERMANENT MESSAGE CONTACT   PHONE (/ Area Code)
Name, Street Address,
City and State of someone
(other than spouse) where
you may always be contacted

EDUCATION → High School and College or University (include City and State) | Attendance FROM MO YR / TO MO YR | UNITS COMPLETED | Major Field | Grade Point Average GRADE / SCALE | Degree Awarded | Date Awarded

List other education or training of significance

CHRONOLOGICAL EMPLOYMENT HISTORY – Account for all time for at least the past ten years, including U.S. Military Service and National Guard. If employed in your own business, give firm name and complete address of a business reference who can verify your activities during this period. If unemployed during any part of this period, list name and complete address of one person, not a relative, who can verify the unemployment period. You may refer to resume if attached; however, all information must be given, including salary breakdown. If professional history extends beyond ten years, please include. Your present employer will not be contacted without your specific permission.   INCOMPLETE APPLICATIONS WILL NOT BE CONSIDERED

SALARY
PER HOUR, WEEK (NO HOUR): MONTH OR YEAR (DO NOT INCLUDE OVERTIME)
START _____ FINAL _____ PER _____

1 PRESENT OR LAST POSITION
COMPANY   FROM (MONTH/YEAR) | TO (MONTH/YEAR)   BASE

ADDRESS (No., Street, City, State and Zip Code)   BONUS

POSITION OR TITLE   AVAILABILITY DATE   FIELD PAY

BRIEFLY DESCRIBE YOUR DUTIES   OTHER (EXPLAIN)

NAME OF IMMEDIATE SUPERVISOR | REASON FOR LEAVING OR WANTING TO LEAVE   TOTAL

2 COMPANY   FROM (MONTH/YEAR) | TO (MONTH/YEAR)   BASE

ADDRESS (No., Street, City, State and Zip Code)   BONUS

POSITION AND DUTIES   FIELD PAY

OTHER (EXPLAIN)

NAME OF IMMEDIATE SUPERVISOR | REASON FOR LEAVING   TOTAL

3

COMPANY

ADDRESS (No., Street, City, State and Zip Code)

POSITION AND DUTIES

NAME OF IMMEDIATE SUPERVISOR

FROM (MONTH/YEAR) | TO (MONTH/YEAR)

BASE
BONUS
FIELD PAY
OTHER (EXPLAIN)
TOTAL

REASON FOR LEAVING

4

COMPANY

ADDRESS (No., Street, City, State and Zip Code)

POSITION AND DUTIES

NAME OF IMMEDIATE SUPERVISOR

FROM (MONTH/YEAR) | TO (MONTH/YEAR)

BASE
BONUS
FIELD PAY
OTHER (EXPLAIN)
TOTAL

REASON FOR LEAVING

5 List additional positions necessary to make this employment record cover ten (10) years or more (continue on separate page if necessary)

MO FROM YR | MO TO YR | COMPANY | ADDRESS | YOUR POSITION | BASE SALARY | PER

PROFESSIONAL REFERENCES: Name five (5) persons in your field whom you know, and whom WE HAVE YOUR PERMISSION TO CONTACT, preferably professional and technical persons with whom you have worked

NAME | HOME ADDRESS | COMPANY OR AFFILIATION | BUSINESS PHONE

LIST OR BRIEFLY DESCRIBE any significant projects, thesis subjects, patent applications or publications to which you have given major effort or for which awards have been granted

BRIEFLY DESCRIBE the type of work for which you are best fitted by virtue of your aptitude, interests, education and experience

FORM LAC 200-3

NOTE – Complete reverse side

127

REQ. NO.

DEPT/ORGN NO.

OCCUPATIONAL CODE

ZERO YEAR | SAL GRD.

MO | FAC | PTS

Type or print (in Ink)

APPLICANT'S NAME   Last   First   Middle

DATE PREPARED

CURRENT ADDRESS – No. and Street

HOME PHONE (Area Code)

City, State and Zip Code

BUSINESS PHONE (Area Code)   EXT.

PERMANENT MESSAGE CONTACT

PHONE (Area Code)

Name, Street Address, City and State of someone (other than spouse) where you may always be contacted

EDUCATION ► High School and College or University (include City and State)

	Attendance		UNITS COMPLETED	Major Field	Grade Point Average		Degree Awarded	Date Awarded
	FROM MO YR	TO MO YR			GRADE	SCALE		

List other education or training of significance

CHRONOLOGICAL EMPLOYMENT HISTORY – Account for all time for at least the past ten years, including U.S. Military Service and National Guard. If employed in your own business, give firm name and complete address of this period. If unemployed during any part of this period, list name and complete address of one person, not a relative, who can verify your activities during the unemployment period. You may refer to resume if attached; however, all information must be given, including salary breakdown. If professional history extends beyond ten years, please include. Your present employer will not be contacted without your specific permission.
INCOMPLETE APPLICATIONS WILL NOT BE CONSIDERED

1 PRESENT OR LAST POSITION
COMPANY

FROM (MONTH/YEAR) TO (MONTH/YEAR)

SALARY:
PER HOUR, WEEK (40 HOUR): MONTH OR YEAR
(DO NOT INCLUDE OVERTIME)

START   FINAL   PER

ADDRESS (No., Street, City, State and Zip Code)

BASE

POSITION OR TITLE

AVAILABILITY DATE

BONUS

FIELD PAY

BRIEFLY DESCRIBE YOUR DUTIES

OTHER (EXPLAIN)

NAME OF IMMEDIATE SUPERVISOR   REASON FOR LEAVING OR WANTING TO LEAVE

TOTAL

2 COMPANY

FROM (MONTH/YEAR) TO (MONTH/YEAR)

BASE

ADDRESS (No., Street, City, State and Zip Code)

BONUS

POSITION AND DUTIES

FIELD PAY

OTHER (EXPLAIN)

NAME OF IMMEDIATE SUPERVISOR   REASON FOR LEAVING

TOTAL

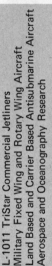

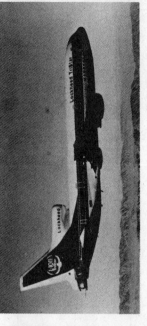

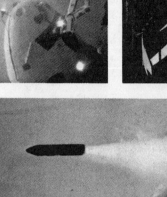

LOCKHEED AIRCRAFT CORPORATION

AN EQUAL OPPORTUNITY EMPLOYER

LOCKHEED-CALIFORNIA COMPANY
P.O. Box 551
Burbank, Calif. 91520

L-1011 TriStar Commercial Jetliners
Military Fixed Wing and Rotary Wing Aircraft
Land Based and Carrier Based Antisubmarine Aircraft
Aerospace and Oceanography Research

LOCKHEED-GEORGIA COMPANY
Marietta, Ga. 30063

Military and Commercial Airlifters
Business Jets
Short Takeoff Research and Design
Aerospace Research

LOCKHEED MISSILES & SPACE COMPANY, INC.
P.O. Box 504
Sunnyvale, Calif. 94088

Strategic Missile Systems
Military and Commercial Space Systems
Communication Satellites
Ground Vehicles
Deep Submersible Vehicles and Systems

LOCKHEED INTERNATIONAL COMPANY
P. O. Box 551
Burbank, Calif. 91520

International Joint Ventures
Foreign Licensing Programs
Overseas Manufacturing Facilities

LOCKHEED AIRCRAFT SERVICE COMPANY
P.O. Box 33
Ontario, Calif. 91764

Aircraft Maintenance. Training Devices.
Electronic and Marine Products and Services
Vehicle Development. Data Recording and
Analysis Systems. Electro-Chemical and
Electro-Mechanical Products

LOCKHEED AIR TERMINAL, INC.
2627 N. Hollywood Way
Burbank, Calif. 91505

Airport Management
Aircraft Fuel Handling
General Aviation Services

LOCKHEED ELECTRONICS COMPANY
U.S. Highway 22
Plainfield, N.J. 07061

Military and Commercial Electronic Systems
Spacecraft and Commercial Instrumentation
Recorders. Computer Memory Systems
and Components. Space Engineering,
Scientific and Technical Support

LOCKHEED PROPULSION COMPANY
P.O. Box 111
Redlands, Calif. 92374

Attack Missile Motors. Solid, Hybrid
and Restartable Pulse Motors.
Launch Escape Motors
Reactor Components. Testing Services

LOCKHEED SHIPBUILDING AND CONSTRUCTION COMPANY
2929 16th Avenue, S.W.
Seattle, Wash. 98134

Shipbuilding, Conversion and Repair
Heavy Construction. Quarry Management
Industrial Cranes and Materials Handling
Equipment

REQ. NO.

DATE PREPARED

OCCUPATIONAL CODE

ORGN. | SAL. GRD.

NO. | FAC | PTS.

Type or Print
(In Ink)

DATE

● APPLICANT'S NAME

Last | First | Middle

● CURRENT ADDRESS – No. and Street

City, State and Zip Code

HOME PHONE (Area Code)

BUSINESS PHONE (Area Code) | EXT.

● PERMANENT MESSAGE CONTACT
Name, Street Address
City, State and Zip
Code of someone
(other than spouse)
where you may always
be contacted

PHONE (Area Code)

● JOB DESIRED (Please indicate)

INDICATE SHIFTS YOU ARE WILLING TO WORK

☐ ANY ☐ DAY ☐ SWING ☐ GRAVE YARD

DO YOU READ BLUEPRINTS? ☐ YES ☐ NO

DO YOU READ SCHEMATICS? ☐ YES ☐ NO

TYPING SPEED | WPM

STENO SPEED | WPM

● EDUCATION – High School, Technical School, Military School, Night School, Trade and Apprenticeships and College or University (include City and State)

Attendance FROM | TO | Major Field | Units Completed | Grade Point Average GRADE — SCALE | Degree Awarded | Date Awarded

MO | YR | MO | YR

List other education
or training of
significance – include
licenses and certificates

● EMPLOYMENT HISTORY – Account for all time for at least the past ten years. Include U.S. and National Guard Military service. If in "own business," give firm name and name and address of a business reference. If unemployed or a housewife, hospitalized, traveling, etc., give complete details, including dates and addresses. Periods of unemployment must be verifiable by personal references. You may refer to a resume if attached, however, all information must be given, including rate of pay and reason for leaving.

INCOMPLETE APPLICATIONS WILL NOT BE CONSIDERED.

PRESENT OR LAST POSITION
FROM (MONTH/YEAR) | TO (MONTH/YEAR) | TIME IN MONTHS | EMPLOYER'S NAME | TYPE OF BUSINESS

1 ADDRESS (No., Street, City, State and Zip Code) | TITLE OF your JOB

BRIEFLY OUTLINE MAJOR DUTIES (work done, tools used, machines operated, etc.)

DATE AVAILABLE TO BEGIN WORK | SUPERVISOR'S NAME | REASON FOR LEAVING | BASE RATE PER HOUR Exclude overtime, field pay, shift bonus, cost of living, differential, and other bonuses

FROM (MONTH/YEAR) | TO (MONTH/YEAR) | TIME IN MONTHS | EMPLOYER'S NAME | TYPE OF BUSINESS

2 ADDRESS (No., Street, City, State and Zip Code) | TITLE OF your JOB

BRIEFLY OUTLINE MAJOR DUTIES (work done, tools used, machines operated, etc.)

SUPERVISOR'S NAME | REASON FOR LEAVING | BASE RATE PER HOUR Exclude overtime, field pay, shift bonus, cost of living, differential, and other bonuses

FROM (MONTH/YEAR) | TO (MONTH/YEAR) | TIME IN MONTHS | EMPLOYER'S NAME | TYPE OF BUSINESS

3 ADDRESS (No., Street, City, State and Zip Code) | TITLE OF your JOB

BRIEFLY OUTLINE MAJOR DUTIES (work done, tools used, machines operated, etc.)

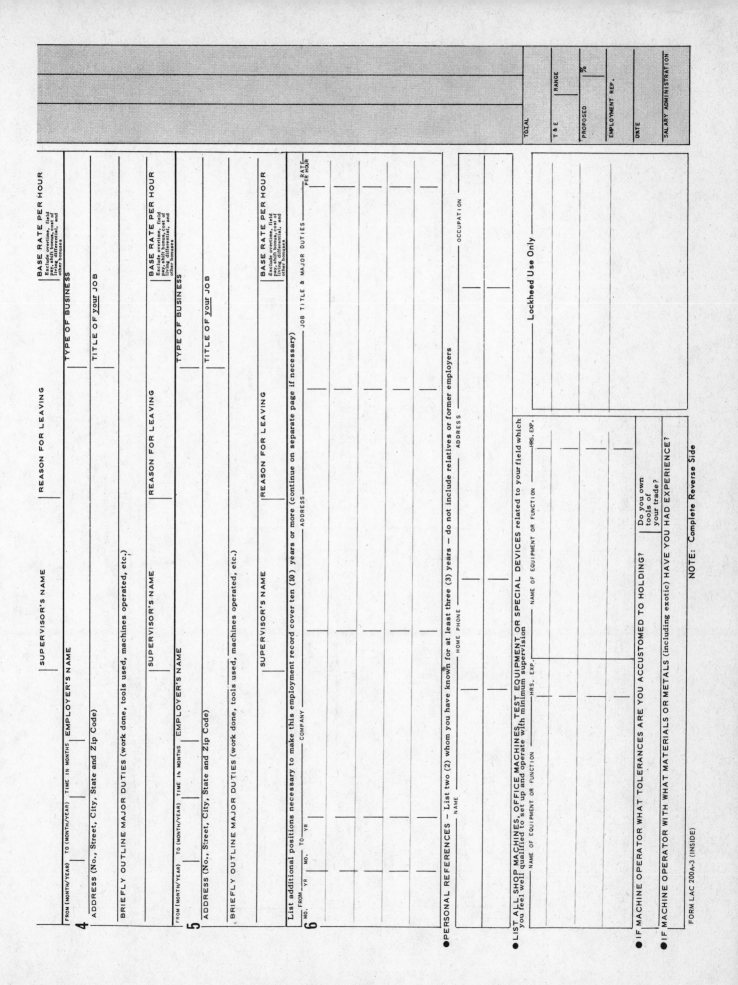

131

IDENTIFICATION

BIRTHDATE   SOCIAL SECURITY NUMBER

Give all previous names by which known.

MEDICAL DATA

Do you have or have you had in the past any physical, visual or mental limitations or defects? Include even those that were temporarily disabling.

☐ Yes ► Describe

☐ No

HEIGHT   WEIGHT

EMERGENCY CONTACT — Person who can be contacted in emergency

NAME

PHONE
(Area Code)

ADDRESS (No., Street, City, State and Zip Code)

U.S. MILITARY SERVICE

BRANCH OF SERVICE | RANK | ENTRY DATE | DISCHARGE DATE | TYPE OF DISCHARGE | ARE YOU UNDER NOTICE TO REPORT FOR DUTY?

PROFESSIONAL ORGANIZATIONS OR ASSOCIATIONS

Do not include Trade Unions and others which indicate the race, religious creed, color, national origin, ancestry or political affiliation of its members.

RELATIVES OR ACQUAINTANCES EMPLOYED BY LOCKHEED (Please list below)

NAME   POSITION   DEPT.   RELATIONSHIP

How did you learn of employment opportunities at Lockheed?

☐ Magazine Ad   ☐ Lockheed Employee
☐ Newspaper Ad   ☐ Other Means

Please name below:

CITIZENSHIP — If employed, can you submit a Birth Certificate or other proof of U.S. citizenship?

NO ☐   YES ☐

If no, do you have a legal right to remain permanently in the U.S.?

NO ☐   YES ☐

Indicate level of most recent clearance, date granted and where employed at that time

SECURITY CLEARANCE

Have you ever had a Security Clearance?

NO ☐   YES ☐

Indicate level of clearance, date when action occurred, by whom and where employed at that time

Have you ever had a Security Clearance suspended, denied or revoked?

NO ☐   YES ☐

HAVE YOU

Ever worked or applied for work at a Lockheed Company?

NO ☐   YES ☐ ► ☐ Worked ☐ Applied

Where and when (Employee No. if applicable)

Ever worked for Lockheed under a different name?

NO ☐   YES ☐

Give name used, where used and explain

Are you, or have you ever been a member of any communist organization or political party or organization which advocates or advocated the overthrow of our constitutional form of government in the United States, or do you have or have you had membership in or affiliation with any group, association or organization which advocated or advocates or lent or lends support to any organization or movement advocating the overthrow of our constitutional form of government in the United States.

WRITE ANSWER ► Yes or No _____
DO NOT TYPE OR PRINT

If yes, name the organization and give complete details below or on separate page

Have you ever been convicted of an offense against the law, or forfeited collateral, or are you now under charges for any offense against the law? Include any convictions by general courts-martial while in military service. (You may omit: (a) traffic violations for which you paid a fine of $25.00 or less: and (b) any offense committed before your 18th birthday which was finally adjudicated in a juvenile court or under a youth offender law.) Include all instances where nolo contender was plead, where bail was forfeited, and where a fine was paid.

Write Yes or No ► If yes, give date, place, charge and disposition below or on separate page

Have you ever been convicted of a crime under another name?

☐ Yes ☐ No

Give name used, where used and explain

Equal opportunity in the hiring, training, transfer, and promotion of its employees, has been a Lockheed policy for many years. To further insure, and strengthen this policy, we have organized an effective "affirmative action" program, with benefits applied fairly and equally to all without regard to race, color, religion, sex, age, or national origin.

— USE THE FOLLOWING SPACE AS REQUIRED —

I hereby certify that the answers given by me to the foregoing questions and statements made are true and correct without consequential omissions of any kind whatsoever. I agree that the companies shall not be liable in any respect if my employment is terminated because of the falsity of statements, answers or omissions made by me in this questionnaire. I agree to submit to physical examination. If employment is obtained under this application I will comply with all orders, rules and regulations of this Company. I also authorize the companies, schools or persons named above to give any information regarding my employment or education, together with any information they may have regarding me whether or not it is on their records. I hereby release said companies, schools or persons from all liability for any damages whatsoever for issuing this information.

READ THE ABOVE STATEMENT AND SIGN APPLICATION HERE: _____

Falsification will disqualify you for employment.

PLEASE SIGN ►

132

Appendix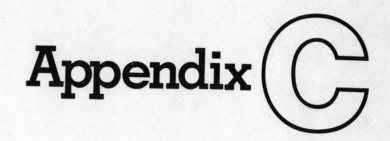

TWO-LETTER STATE ABBREVIATIONS

Alabama	AL	Kentucky	KY	Ohio	OH
Alaska	AK	Louisiana	LA	Oklahoma	OK
Arizona	AZ	Maine	ME	Oregon	OR
Arkansas	AR	Maryland	MD	Pennsylvania	PA
California	CA	Massachusetts	MA	Puerto Rico	PR
Colorado	CO	Michigan	MI	Rhode Island	RI
Connecticut	CT	Minnesota	MN	South Carolina	SC
Delaware	DE	Mississippi	MS	South Dakota	SD
District of Columbia	DC	Missouri	MO	Tennessee	TN
Florida	FL	Montana	MT	Texas	TX
Georgia	GA	Nebraska	NB	Utah	UT
Guam	GU	Nevada	NV	Vermont	VT
Hawaii	HI	New Hampshire	NH	Virginia	VA
Idaho	ID	New Jersey	NJ	Virgin Islands	VI
Illinois	IL	New Mexico	NM	Washington	WA
Indiana	IN	New York	NY	West Virginia	WV
Iowa	IA	North Carolina	NC	Wisconsin	WI
Kansas	KS	North Dakota	ND	Wyoming	WY

Bibliography

WRITTEN COMMUNICATION

Angel, Juvenal L. *Specialized Resumes for Executives and Professionals*. New York: Monarch Press, 1967.

Angel, Juvenal L. *Why and How to Prepare an Effective Resume*, rev. ed. New York: World Trade Academy Press, 1972.

Barr, Doris W. *Writing, Listening, Speaking for Business & Professional Students*. Belmont, CA: Wadsworth Publishing Co., Inc., 1972.

Boll, C. R. "Do's and Don't's of Executive Resumes." *Dun's Review*, 95 (February 1970), 47-48.

Bonner, William H. *Better Business Writing*. Homewood, IL: Richard D. Irwin, Inc., 1974.

Bromage, Mary C. *Writing for Business*. Ann Arbor, MI: University of Michigan Press, 1965.

Camp, G., et al. *Writing Sentences and Paragraphs*. Reading, MA: Addison-Wesley Publishing Co., Inc., 1973.

Corbett, Edward P. *The Little English Handbook: Choices and Conventions*. New York: John Wiley & Sons, Inc., 1973.

Crews, Frederick. *The Random House Handbook*. New York: Random House, Inc., 1974.

Dawe, Jessamon, and William J. Lord, Jr. *Functional Business Communication*, 2nd ed. Englewood Cliffs, NJ: Prentice-Hall, Inc., 1974.

Elfenbein, Julien, ed. *Handbook of Business Form Letters and Forms*. New York: Monarch Press, 1974.

Ewing, David W. *Writing for Results*. New York: John Wiley & Sons, Inc., 1974.

Faulkner, Claude W. *Writing Good Sentences*. New York: Charles Scribner's Sons, 1973.

Glorfeld, Louis E., et al. *A Concise Guide for Writers*, 3rd ed. Holt, Rinehart, and Winston, Inc., 1974.

Goeller, Carl. *Writing to Communicate*. New York: Doubleday & Co., Inc., 1974.

Himstreet, William C., and Murlin W. Baty. *Business Communications*, 4th ed. Belmont, CA:
Wadsworth Publishing Co., Inc., 1972.

Hodges, John C., and Mary E. Whitten, eds. *Harbrace College Handbook*, 7th ed. New York: Harcourt,
Brace & World, Inc., 1972.

Huseman, Richard C., *et al*. *Readings in Interpersonal Organizational Communication*, 2nd ed.
Boston: Holbrook Press, 1973.

Irmscher, William F., and Mary L. Morr. *The Holt Guide to English*. New York: Holt, Rinehart, and
Winston, Inc., 1972.

Janes, Harold D. "The Cover Letter and Resume." *Personnel Journal*, 48 (September 1969), 732-33.

Janis, Harold J. *Writing & Communication in Business*, 2nd ed. New York: Macmillan Publishing Co.,
1973.

Janis, Harold J., and Howard R. Dressner. *Business Writing*. New York: Barnes & Noble, Inc., 1972

Lawrence, Nelda R. *Writing Communication in Business & Industry*, 2nd ed. Englewood Cliffs, NJ:
Prentice-Hall, Inc., 1974.

Lesikar, Raymond V. *Business Communication: Theory and Application*, rev. ed. Homewood, IL:
Richard D. Irwin, Inc., 1972.

Lindaurer, Jacqueline S. *Writing in Business*. New York: Macmillan Publishing Co., 1971.

McCrimmon, James M. *Writing with a Purpose: 1976 Impression*, 6th ed. New York: Houghton Mifflin
Co., 1976.

Menning, Jack H., and C. W. Wilkinson. *Communication Through Letters and Reports*, 5th ed.
Homewood, IL: Richard D. Irwin, Inc., 1972.

Miller, Shirley M., ed. *Webster's New World Thirty-Three-Thousand Word Book*, rev. ed. Cleveland,
OH: Collins, Williams & World Publishing Co., 1971.

Monaghan, Patrick. *Writing Letters that Sell You, Your Ideas, Products & Services*. New York:
Fairchild Publishers, Inc., 1968.

Nurnberg, Maxwell. *Questions You Always Wanted to Ask About English: But Were Afraid to Raise
Your Hand*. New York: Washington Square Press, 1972.

Perham, J. C. "What's Wrong with Executive Resumes?" *Dun's Review*, 105 (May 1975), 50-52.

Perrin, Porter G., and Wilma R. Ebbitt. *Writer's Guide & Index to English*, 5th ed. Glenview, IL:
Scott, Foresman and Co., 1972.

Rubinstein, S. Leonard. *Writing: A Habit of Mind*. Dubuque, IA: William C. Brown Co., 1972.

Ryan, Charles W. *Writing for Government & Industry*. New York: John Wiley & Sons, Inc., 1974

Seation, A. G. *Writer's Dictionary*. New York: St. Martin Press, Inc., 1973.

Sharp, Henry, ed. *Follett Vest-Pocket Word Divider: 50,000 Words and 3,400 Variants Spelled, Pronounced, and Divided*. Chicago: Follett Publishing Co., 1964.

Shykind, Maury. *Resumes for Executive Job Hunters*. New York: Arco Publishing Co., Inc., 1971.

Strand, Stanley, and E. C. Gruber. *Resumes for Better Jobs*. New York: Monarch Press, 1974.

Strunk, William, Jr. and E. B. White. *The Elements of Style*, 2nd ed. New York: Macmillan Publishing Co., 1972.

Wells, Walter. *Communication in Business*. Belmont, CA: Wadsworth Publishing Co., Inc., 1968.

White, Edward M. *Writer's Control of Tone*. New York: W. W. Norton & Co., Inc., 1970.

Wilkins, James H., and Donald L. Caruth. *Lexicon of American Business Terms*. New York: Monarch Press, 1974.

Wilkinson, C. W., *et al. Writing for Business*, 4th ed. Homewood, IL: Richard D. Irwin, Inc., 1966.

Writing Skills One: A Program for Self-Instruction. New York: McGraw-Hill, Inc., 1970.

Writing Skills Two: A Program for Self-Instruction. New York: McGraw-Hill, Inc., 1970.

THE EMPLOYMENT PROCESS

Azeuedo, R. E. "Scientists, Engineers, and the Job Search Process." *California Management Review*, 17 (Winter 1974), 40-49.

Bannon, B. A. "Everything a Woman Needs to Know to Earn What She's Worth." *Publishers Weekly*, 204 (September 10, 1973), 34.

Bellotto, S. "New Opportunities in the Job Market for Managers." *Administrative Management*, 31 (September 1970), 28-31.

Chamberlin, A. "Executive Odyssey: Looking for a Job at Fifty-Five." *Fortune*, 90 (November 1974), 192-195.

Clarke, J. R. "Landing That Right Executive Job." *Management Review*, 64 (August 1975), 31-36.

Dunnette, Marvin D. *Personnel Selection and Placement*. Belmont, CA: Brooks/Cole Publishing Co., 1966.

Dyer, L. D. "Managerial Job Seeking: Methods and Techniques (Forty Plus)." *Monthly Labor Review*, 95 (December 1972), 29-30.

"Finding a Job in the Recession." *Business Week* (January 13, 1975), 101-106.

French, Wendell L. *The Personnel Management Process: Human Resources Administration*, 3rd ed. Boston: Houghton Mifflin Co., 1974.

Hoefler, D. C. "Selling Your Greatest Asset: You." *Electronic News*, 14 (December 1, 1969), 16.

"Job Hunting: Sell Yourself." *Sales Management*, 110 (June 11, 1973), 12.

Liebers, Arthur. *How to Pass Employment Tests*, 5th ed. New York: Arco Publishing Co., 1971.

Marshall, Austin. *How to Get a Better Job*. New York: Hawthorn Books, Inc., 1964.

Mies, W. E. "Finding a Job in Today's Tighter Market—Experts Offer Some Tips." *Pulp & Paper*, 49 (April 1975), 110-12.

Naylor, H. "I'm Honey—Hire Me." *Advertising Age*, 44 (September 17, 1973), 48 ff.

Pell, Arthur R. *The College Graduate Guide to Job Finding*. New York: Monarch Press, 1974.

"Personal Business (Job Hunting)." *Business Week* (March 23, 1974), 73-74.

Peskin, Dean B. *The Art of Job Hunting*. Cleveland, OH: World Publishing Co., 1967.

"Publisher Tells Students How to Apply for Jobs." *Editor & Publisher*, 104 (May 1, 1971), 23.

Sobczak, T. V. "Systems Approach to Job Hunting." *Computers and Automation*, 20 (August 1971), 31-35.

Stevens, D. W. "Job Search Techniques: A New Index of Effectiveness." *Quarterly Review of Economics and Business*, 12 (Summer 1972), 99-103.

Sussman, P. E. "Executive Job-Hunting: It's Still a Tough Market." *Financial Executive*, 42 (February 1974), 20-24.

Tanner, T. "New Ways to Find a Job." *Industrial Research*, 11 (June 1969), 54-56.

Welch, W. F. "Professional Approach to Job Hunting." *Public Relations Journal*, 28 (October 1972), 22-24.

Wright, R. P. "Ten Steps to a New Job." *International Management*, 27 (September 1972), 58.

INTERVIEWING

Balinsky, Benjamin, and Ruth Burger. *The Executive Interview: A Bridge to People*. New York: Harper & Row, 1959.

Basset, Glenn A. *Practical Interviewing: A Handbook for Managers*. New York: American Management Association, 1965.

Bermosk, Loretta, and Mary J. Mordane. *Interviewing in Nursing*. New York: Macmillan Publishing Co., 1973.

Black, James M. *How to Get Results from Interviewing: A Practical Guide for Operating Management*. New York: McGraw-Hill, Inc., 1970.

Carlson, Robert E. "Effects of Application Sample on Ratings of Valid Information in an Employment Setting." *Journal of Applied Psychology*, 54 (1970), 217-22.

Carlson, Robert E. "Selection Interview Decisions; The Effect of Mode Applicant Presentation on Some Outcome Measures." *Personnel Psychology*, 21 (1968), 193-207.

Carlson, Robert E., D. P. Schwab, and H. G. Henneman. "Agreement Among Selection Interview Styles." *Journal of Industrial Psychology*, 5 (1970), 8-17.

Downs, Calvin W. "Perceptions and the Selection Interview." *Personnel Administration* (May-June 1969), 8.

Fenlason, Ann. Essentials in Interviewing, rev. by G. B. Ferguson and C. Abrahamson. New York: Harper & Row, 1962.

Ford, Guy B. *Building a Winning Team*. New York: American Management Association, 1964.

Harral, Stewart. *Keys to Successful Interviewing*. Norman, OK: University of Oklahoma Press, 1954.

Holm, Donald Jr. *Job Interviews*. Los Angeles: Lucas Brothers, 1974.

Gorden, Raymond L. *Interviewing Strategy, Techniques, and Tactics*, rev. ed. Homewood, IL: Dorsey Press, 1975.

Huguenard, T., E. B. Sager, and L. W. Ferguson. "Interview Time, Interview Set, and Interview Outcome." *Perceptual and Motor Skills*, 31 (December 1970), 831-36.

Kephart, Newell C. *The Employment Interview in Industry*. New York: McGraw-Hill, Inc., 1952.

Martin, Richard. "Recruiter Revisited." *The Wall Street Journal* (10 April 1972 Sec. 70), 1, 14.

Pell, Arthur B. *Recruiting and Selecting Personnel*. New York: Monarch Press, 1974.

Peskin, Dean B. *Human Behavior and Employment Interviewing*. New York: American Management Association, 1971.

Schubert, Margaret. *Interviewing in Social Work Practice: An Introduction*. New York: Council on Social Work Education, 1971.

Schwab, D. P. "Why Interview? A Critique." *Personnel Journal*, 48, (1969), 126-29.

Shouksmith, George. *Assessment Through Interviewing*. London: Pergamon Press, 1968.

Stewart, Charles J., and William B. Cash, Jr. *Interviewing: Principles and Practices*. Dubuque, IA: William C. Brown Co., 1974.

Taylor, Vernon R. "A Hard Look at the Selection Interview." *Public Personnel Review* (July 1969), 149.

Ungerson, Bernard, ed. *Recruitment Handbook: A Standard Text for Personnel Managers*. New York: Beekman Publishers, 1970.

Weinland, James D., and Margaret V. Gross. *Personnel Interviewing*. New York: Ronald Press, 1952.

OCCUPATIONAL GUIDES

Angel, Juvenal L. *Employment Opportunities for Men and Women After Sixty*. New York: World Trade Academy Press, 1969.

Angel, Juvenal L. *Employment Opportunities for the Handicapped*. New York: Monarch Press, 1969.

Angel, Juvenal L. *Looking for Employment in Foreign Countries: Reference Handbook*, 6th ed. New York: World Trade Academy Press, 1972.

Angel, Juvenal L. *Matching Armed Forces Training to Civilian Jobs*. New York: World Trade Academy Press, 1971.

Angel, Juvenal L. *Matching College Men to Jobs*. New York: World Trade Academy Press, 1971.

Angel, Juvenal L. *Matching College Women to Jobs*. New York: Monarch Press, 1970.

Angel, Juvenal L. *Matching High School Graduates to Jobs*. New York: World Trade Academy Press, 1971.

Angel, Juvenal L. *Matching Technicians to Jobs*. New York: World Trade Academy Press, 1971.

Angel, Juvenal L. *Modern Vocational Trends Reference Handbook*. New York: Monarch Press, 1969.

Angel, Juvenal L. *Occupations for Men and Women After 45*, 3rd rev. ed. New York: World Trade Academy Press, 1964.

Angel, Juvenal L. *Selective Guide to Overseas Employment*. New York: Regents Publishing Co., 1968.

Angel, Juvenal L. *Student's Guide to Occupational Opportunities and Their Lifetime Earnings*. New York: World Trade Academy Press, 1967.

Goldenthal, Allan B. *Teenage Employment Guide*. New York: Monarch Press, 1974.

Goldenthal, Allan B. *Your Career Selection Guide*. New York: Monarch Press, 1974.

Hopke, William E. *Encyclopedia of Careers and Vocational Guidance*, 3rd ed., 2 vols. Garden City, NY: Doubleday & Co., Inc., 1975.

Pell, Arthur, and Wilma Rogalin. *Women's Guide to Management Positions*. New York: Simon & Schuster, Inc., 1975.

U.S. Department of Labor, Labor Statistics Bureau. *Jobs for Which College Education Is Usually Required*. Washington, DC: Government Printing Office, 1973.

U.S. Department of Labor, Labor Statistics Bureau. *Occupational Outlook Handbook*. Washington, DC: Government Printing Office, 1974.

U.S. Department of Labor, Labor Statistics Bureau. *Occupational Outlook for College Graduates 1972-73*. Washington, DC: Government Printing Office, 1972.

U.S. Department of Labor, Women's Bureau. *Careers for Women in the 70's (with a list of references)*. Washington, DC: Government Printing Office, 1973.

U.S. Department of Labor, Women's Bureau. *Selected Sources of Career Information*. Washington, DC: Government Printing Office, 1974.

Whitfield, Edwin and Richard Hoover. *Guide to Careers Through Vocational Training*. San Diego, CA: Robert R. Knapp Co., 1968.

Who's Hiring Who: The Journal of Jobs. Washington, DC: Human Resources Press. Issued annually.

Wolfbein, Seymour L. *Occupational Information: A Career Guidance View*. Philadelphia, PA: Philadelphia Book Co., Inc., 1968.

SPECIAL INFORMATION

AAUP Bulletin. Washington, DC: Association of University Professors. Issued quarterly.

ABCA Bulletin. Urbana, IL: American Business Communication Association. Issued quarterly.

ASUC Annual. Brooklyn, NY: Association of State Colleges, and Universities Communications, and Service Center.

Accountants' Index. New York: American Institute of Certified Public Accountants. Issued annually.

Alexander, Raphael, ed. *Business Pamphlets and Information Sources*. New York: Exceptional Books, 1967.

Angel, Juvenal L. *Directory of American Firms Operating in Foreign Countries*, 8th ed. New York: Simon & Schuster, Inc., 1973.

Angel, Juvenal L. *Directory of Foreign Firms Operating in the United States*. New York: World Trade Academy Press, 1971.

Angel, Juvenal L. *Directory of Intercorporate Ownership: Who Owns Whom in America*, 2 vols. New York: World Trade Academy Press, 1974.

Angel, Juvenal L. *Directory of International Agencies*. New York: Monarch Press, 1970.

Angel, Juvenal L. *Directory of Professional and Occupational Licensing in the United States*. New York: Monarch Press, 1969.

Angel, Juvenal L. *Handbook of International Business and Investment Facts and Information Sources*. New York: World Trade Academy Press, 1967.

Angel, Juvenal L. *International Marketing Guides for Technical, Management and Other Consultants*. New York: World Trade Academy Press, 1971.

Applied Science and Technology Index (formerly *Industrial Arts Index*). New York: H. W. Wilson Co. Issued quarterly, monthly, with quarterly and annual cumulation.

Arts Index. New York: H. W. Wilson Co.

Ayer's Directory of Newspapers and Periodicals. Philadelphia: Ayer's Press. Issued annually.

Belson, W. A., and B. A. Thompson. *Bibliography on Methods of Social and Business Research*. New York: Halsted Press, 1973.

Biological and Agricultural Index. New York: H. W. Wilson Co., 1967. Issued annually.

Broom, Halsey N., and Justin G. Longenecker. *Small Business Management*, 3rd ed. Cincinnati, OH: South-Western Publishing Co., 1971.

Business Periodicals Index. New York: H. W. Wilson Co. Issued monthly, with annual cumulation.

College Placement Council. *College Placement Annual*. Bethlehem, PA: College Placement Council. Issued quarterly.

Education Index. New York: H. W. Wilson Co. Issued monthly, with annual cumulation.

Encyclopedia of Business Information Sources. Detroit, MI: Gale Research Co., 1970.

Engineering Index. New York: Engineering Index, Inc. Issued annually.

Fiske, Margaret, ed. *Encyclopedia of Associations*, 9th ed., 3 vols. Detroit, MI: Gale Research Co., 1975.

Funk and Scott's Index of Corporations and Industries. Detroit, MI: Funk & Scott Publishing Co. Issued weekly, monthly, and annual cumulation.

Gebbie Press House Magazine Directory, 8th ed. Burlington, IA: National Research Bureau, Inc., 1974.

Guide to American Directories. New York: B. Klein & Co. Issued irregularly.

Houston, Samuel R., *et al.*, eds. *Methods and Techniques of Business Research*. New York: Mss Information Corp., 1973

Industrial Arts Index. See Applied Science and Technology Index.

International Bibliography of Directories, 5th ed. New York: R. R. Bowker Co., 1973.

Johnson, Herbert W. *How to Use the Business Library with Sources of Business Information*, 4th ed. Cincinnati, OH: South-Western Publishing Co., 1973.

Koontz, Harold, and Cyril O'Donnell. *Principles of Management*, 5th ed. New York: McGraw-Hill, Inc., 1972.

Kraft, K. C. *Directory of United States Employers*. New York: Monarch Press, 1974.

McCormick, Mona. *The New York Times Guide to Reference Materials*. New York: Popular Library, 1972.

Massie, Joseph L. *Essentials of Management*, 2nd ed. Englewood Cliffs, NJ: Prentice-Hall, Inc., 1970.

Moody's Bank & Finance Manual. New York: Moody's Investors Service. Issued annually, weekly supplements.

Moody's Industrial Manual. New York: Moody's Investors Service. Issued annually, weekly supplements.

National Directory of Employment Services. Detroit: Gale Research Co. Issued irregularly.

Poor's Register of Directors and Executives of the United States and Canada. New York: Standard and Poor's Corporation. Issued annually.

Prince, Martin, ed. *Commercial Directories of the United States*. Originally titled: *Directory of Commercial Directories and Annual Publications*. Cedarhurst, NY: WMP Publishers, 1972.

Rummel, Francis J. and Wesley C. Ballaine. *Research Methodology in Business*. New York: Harper & Row, 1963.

Scientific and Technical Societies of the U.S., 8th ed. Washington DC: National Academy of Science, 1968.

Small Business Administration. *Small Business Bibliography*. Washington DC: Government Printing Office, 1966.

Smith, George M. and Herbert J. Smith. *World Wide Business Publications Directory*. New York: Monarch Press, 1974.

Sololik, Stanley L. *The Personnel Process: Line and Staff Dimensions in Managing People at Work*. Scranton, PA: International Textbook, 1970.

Standard Directory of Newsletters. New York: Oxbridge Publishing Co., 1972.

Standard Periodical Directory. New York: Oxbridge Publishing Co., Inc. Issued irregularly.

Standard Rate and Data Guide: Business Publication Rates and Data. Skokie, IL: Standard Rate and Data Services, Inc. Issued monthly.

Thomas' Register of American Manufacturers. New York: Thomas Publishing Co. Issued annually.

Trade Directories of the World. Queens Village, NY: Croner Publishers, 1971.

Ulrich's Periodicals Directory. New York: R. R. Bowker Co. Issued annually.

Wasserman, Paul, ed. *Statistics Sources: A Subject Guide to Data on Industrial, Business, Social, Educational, Financial, and other Topics for the United States and Selected Foreign Countries*, 4th ed. Detroit, MI: Gale Research Co., 1974.

Who's Who. New York: St. Martin Press. Issued annually.

Writer's Market. Cincinnati, OH: Writer's Digest. Issued annually.

Index